C000136258

Dispute Resolution
Complete Self-Assessment G

The guidance in this Self-Assessment ~~is based on Dispute Resolution~~ best practices and standards in business process architecture, design and quality management. The guidance is also based on the professional judgment of the individual collaborators listed in the Acknowledgments.

Table of Contents

About The Art of Service

The Art of Service, Business Process Architects since 2000, is dedicated to helping stakeholders achieve excellence.

Defining, designing, creating, and implementing a process to solve a stakeholders challenge or meet an objective is the most valuable role… In EVERY group, company, organization and department.

Unless you're talking a one-time, single-use project, there should be a process. Whether that process is managed and implemented by humans, AI, or a combination of the two, it needs to be designed by someone with a complex enough perspective to ask the right questions.

Someone capable of asking the right questions and step back and say, 'What are we really trying to accomplish here? And is there a different way to look at it?'

With The Art of Service's Standard Requirements Self-Assessments, we empower people who can do just that — whether their title is marketer, entrepreneur, manager, salesperson, consultant, Business Process Manager, executive assistant, IT Manager, CIO etc... —they are the people who rule the future. They are people who watch the process as it happens, and ask the right questions to make the process work better.

Contact us when you need any support with this Self-Assessment and any help with templates, blue-prints and examples of standard documents you might need:

http://theartofservice.com
service@theartofservice.com

Acknowledgments

This checklist was developed under the auspices of The Art of Service, chaired by Gerardus Blokdyk.

Representatives from several client companies participated in the preparation of this Self-Assessment.

In addition, we are thankful for the design and printing services provided.

Included Resources - how to access

Included with your purchase of the book is the Dispute Resolution Self-Assessment Spreadsheet Dashboard which contains all questions and Self-Assessment areas and auto-generates insights, graphs, and project RACI planning - all with examples to get you started right away.

How? Simply send an email to
access@theartofservice.com
with this books' title in the subject to get the Dispute Resolution Self Assessment Tool right away.

You will receive the following contents with New and Updated specific criteria:

- The latest quick edition of the book in PDF

- The latest complete edition of the book in PDF, which criteria correspond to the criteria in...

- The Self-Assessment Excel Dashboard, and...

- Example pre-filled Self-Assessment Excel Dashboard to get familiar with results generation

- In-depth specific Checklists covering the topic

- Project management checklists and templates to assist with implementation

INCLUDES LIFETIME SELF ASSESSMENT UPDATES

Every self assessment comes with Lifetime Updates and Lifetime Free Updated Books. Lifetime Updates is an industry-first feature which allows you to receive verified self assessment updates, ensuring you always have the most accurate information at your fingertips.

Get it now- you will be glad you did - do it now, before you forget.

Send an email to **access@theartofservice.com** with this books' title in the subject to get the Dispute Resolution Self Assessment Tool right away.

Your feedback is invaluable to us

If you recently bought this book, we would love to hear from you! You can do this by writing a review on amazon (or the online store where you purchased this book) about your last purchase! As part of our continual service improvement process, we love to hear real client experiences and feedback.

How does it work?
To post a review on Amazon, just log in to your account and click on the Create Your Own Review button (under Customer Reviews) of the relevant product page. You can find examples of product reviews in Amazon. If you purchased from another online store, simply follow their procedures.

What happens when I submit my review?
Once you have submitted your review, send us an email at review@theartofservice.com with the link to your review so we can properly thank you for your feedback.

Purpose of this Self-Assessment

This Self-Assessment has been developed to improve understanding of the requirements and elements of Dispute Resolution, based on best practices and standards in business process architecture, design and quality management.

It is designed to allow for a rapid Self-Assessment to determine how closely existing management practices and procedures correspond to the elements of the Self-Assessment.

The criteria of requirements and elements of Dispute Resolution have been rephrased in the format of a Self-Assessment questionnaire, with a seven-criterion scoring system, as explained in this document.

In this format, even with limited background knowledge of

Dispute Resolution, a manager can quickly review existing operations to determine how they measure up to the standards. This in turn can serve as the starting point of a 'gap analysis' to identify management tools or system elements that might usefully be implemented in the organization to help improve overall performance.

How to use the Self-Assessment

On the following pages are a series of questions to identify to what extent your Dispute Resolution initiative is complete in comparison to the requirements set in standards.

To facilitate answering the questions, there is a space in front of each question to enter a score on a scale of '1' to '5'.

1 Strongly Disagree

2 Disagree

3 Neutral

4 Agree

5 Strongly Agree

Read the question and rate it with the following in front of mind:

'In my belief, the answer to this question is clearly defined'.

There are two ways in which you can choose to interpret this statement;
1. how aware are you that the answer to the question is clearly defined
2. for more in-depth analysis you can choose to gather

evidence and confirm the answer to the question. This obviously will take more time, most Self-Assessment users opt for the first way to interpret the question and dig deeper later on based on the outcome of the overall Self-Assessment.

A score of '1' would mean that the answer is not clear at all, where a '5' would mean the answer is crystal clear and defined. Leave emtpy when the question is not applicable or you don't want to answer it, you can skip it without affecting your score. Write your score in the space provided.

After you have responded to all the appropriate statements in each section, compute your average score for that section, using the formula provided, and round to the nearest tenth. Then transfer to the corresponding spoke in the Dispute Resolution Scorecard on the second next page of the Self-Assessment.

Your completed Dispute Resolution Scorecard will give you a clear presentation of which Dispute Resolution areas need attention.

Dispute Resolution Scorecard Example

Example of how the finalized Scorecard can look like:

Dispute Resolution Scorecard

Your Scores:

BEGINNING OF THE SELF-ASSESSMENT:

CRITERION #1: RECOGNIZE

INTENT: Be aware of the need for change. Recognize that there is an unfavorable variation, problem or symptom.

In my belief, the answer to this question is clearly defined:

5 Strongly Agree

4 Agree

3 Neutral

2 Disagree

1 Strongly Disagree

1. What should be considered when identifying available resources, constraints, and deadlines?
<--- Score

2. What is the smallest subset of the problem you can usefully solve?
<--- Score

3. How are you going to measure success?

<--- Score

4. Does your organization need more Dispute Resolution education?
<--- Score

5. Do you need to avoid or amend any Dispute Resolution activities?
<--- Score

6. What training and capacity building actions are needed to implement proposed reforms?
<--- Score

7. Have you identified your Dispute Resolution key performance indicators?
<--- Score

8. Are problem definition and motivation clearly presented?
<--- Score

9. When a Dispute Resolution manager recognizes a problem, what options are available?
<--- Score

10. Are there any specific expectations or concerns about the Dispute Resolution team, Dispute Resolution itself?
<--- Score

11. Which information does the Dispute Resolution business case need to include?
<--- Score

12. What is the Dispute Resolution problem

definition? What do you need to resolve?
<--- Score

13. What are the minority interests and what amount of minority interests can be recognized?
<--- Score

14. Is it clear when you think of the day ahead of you what activities and tasks you need to complete?
<--- Score

15. How are the Dispute Resolution's objectives aligned to the group's overall stakeholder strategy?
<--- Score

16. Who defines the rules in relation to any given issue?
<--- Score

17. Will new equipment/products be required to facilitate Dispute Resolution delivery, for example is new software needed?
<--- Score

18. What prevents you from making the changes you know will make you a more effective Dispute Resolution leader?
<--- Score

19. What situation(s) led to this Dispute Resolution Self Assessment?
<--- Score

20. Will a response program recognize when a crisis occurs and provide some level of response?
<--- Score

21. What information do users need?
<--- Score

22. How do you assess your Dispute Resolution workforce capability and capacity needs, including skills, competencies, and staffing levels?
<--- Score

23. What activities does the governance board need to consider?
<--- Score

24. Who else hopes to benefit from it?
<--- Score

25. What extra resources will you need?
<--- Score

26. As a sponsor, customer or management, how important is it to meet goals, objectives?
<--- Score

27. What vendors make products that address the Dispute Resolution needs?
<--- Score

28. Can management personnel recognize the monetary benefit of Dispute Resolution?
<--- Score

29. Are there recognized Dispute Resolution problems?
<--- Score

30. Consider your own Dispute Resolution project,

what types of organizational problems do you think might be causing or affecting your problem, based on the work done so far?

<--- Score

31. How can auditing be a preventative security measure?

<--- Score

32. What do you need to start doing?

<--- Score

33. Does Dispute Resolution create potential expectations in other areas that need to be recognized and considered?

<--- Score

34. What would happen if Dispute Resolution weren't done?

<--- Score

35. Do you have/need 24-hour access to key personnel?

<--- Score

36. Think about the people you identified for your Dispute Resolution project and the project responsibilities you would assign to them, what kind of training do you think they would need to perform these responsibilities effectively?

<--- Score

37. Are you dealing with any of the same issues today as yesterday? What can you do about this?

<--- Score

38. What needs to be done?
<--- Score

39. What tools and technologies are needed for a custom Dispute Resolution project?
<--- Score

40. Are employees recognized or rewarded for performance that demonstrates the highest levels of integrity?
<--- Score

41. Who needs to know about Dispute Resolution?
<--- Score

42. Do you need different information or graphics?
<--- Score

43. Will it solve real problems?
<--- Score

44. Are controls defined to recognize and contain problems?
<--- Score

45. What are the timeframes required to resolve each of the issues/problems?
<--- Score

46. What is the problem or issue?
<--- Score

47. What problems are you facing and how do you consider Dispute Resolution will circumvent those obstacles?
<--- Score

48. Who needs what information?
<--- Score

49. What are the expected benefits of Dispute Resolution to the stakeholder?
<--- Score

50. How much are sponsors, customers, partners, stakeholders involved in Dispute Resolution? In other words, what are the risks, if Dispute Resolution does not deliver successfully?
<--- Score

51. Do you know what you need to know about Dispute Resolution?
<--- Score

52. Is the need for organizational change recognized?
<--- Score

53. Will Dispute Resolution deliverables need to be tested and, if so, by whom?
<--- Score

54. What does Dispute Resolution success mean to the stakeholders?
<--- Score

55. To what extent does each concerned units management team recognize Dispute Resolution as an effective investment?
<--- Score

56. What are the stakeholder objectives to be achieved with Dispute Resolution?

<--- Score

57. To what extent would your organization benefit from being recognized as a award recipient?
<--- Score

58. For your Dispute Resolution project, identify and describe the business environment, is there more than one layer to the business environment?
<--- Score

59. How do you identify the kinds of information that you will need?
<--- Score

60. Looking at each person individually – does every one have the qualities which are needed to work in this group?
<--- Score

61. What else needs to be measured?
<--- Score

62. How does it fit into your organizational needs and tasks?
<--- Score

63. Are there any revenue recognition issues?
<--- Score

64. Are your goals realistic? Do you need to redefine your problem? Perhaps the problem has changed or maybe you have reached your goal and need to set a new one?
<--- Score

65. Are there Dispute Resolution problems defined?
<--- Score

66. How do you take a forward-looking perspective in identifying Dispute Resolution research related to market response and models?
<--- Score

67. What are your needs in relation to Dispute Resolution skills, labor, equipment, and markets?
<--- Score

68. Who are your key stakeholders who need to sign off?
<--- Score

Add up total points for this section:
_ _ _ _ _ = Total points for this section

Divided by: _ _ _ _ _ _ (number of statements answered) = _ _ _ _ _ _
Average score for this section

Transfer your score to the Dispute Resolution Index at the beginning of the Self-Assessment.

CRITERION #2: DEFINE:

INTENT: Formulate the stakeholder problem. Define the problem, needs and objectives.

In my belief, the answer to this question is clearly defined:

5 Strongly Agree

4 Agree

3 Neutral

2 Disagree

1 Strongly Disagree

1. Has your scope been defined?
<--- Score

2. Is there a completed SIPOC representation, describing the Suppliers, Inputs, Process, Outputs, and Customers?
<--- Score

3. What are the compelling stakeholder reasons for

embarking on Dispute Resolution?
<--- Score

4. Are audit criteria, scope, frequency and methods
defined?
<--- Score

5. Has everyone on the team, including the team
leaders, been properly trained?
<--- Score

6. Is a fully trained team formed, supported, and
committed to work on the Dispute Resolution
improvements?
<--- Score

7. Is there a clear Dispute Resolution case definition?
<--- Score

8. What sort of initial information to gather?
<--- Score

9. The political context: who holds power?
<--- Score

10. Why are you doing Dispute Resolution and what is
the scope?
<--- Score

11. If substitutes have been appointed, have they
been briefed on the Dispute Resolution goals and
received regular communications as to the progress
to date?
<--- Score

12. How is the team tracking and documenting its

work?
<--- Score

13. Do you have a Dispute Resolution success story or case study ready to tell and share?
<--- Score

14. How are consistent Dispute Resolution definitions important?
<--- Score

15. How can the value of Dispute Resolution be defined?
<--- Score

16. What Dispute Resolution requirements should be gathered?
<--- Score

17. Has anyone else (internal or external to the group) attempted to solve this problem or a similar one before? If so, what knowledge can be leveraged from these previous efforts?
<--- Score

18. Scope of sensitive information?
<--- Score

19. Have specific policy objectives been defined?
<--- Score

20. Has a team charter been developed and communicated?
<--- Score

21. Is Dispute Resolution required?

<--- Score

22. What critical content must be communicated –
who, what, when, where, and how?
<--- Score

23. Is the scope of Dispute Resolution defined?
<--- Score

24. Is the current 'as is' process being followed? If not,
what are the discrepancies?
<--- Score

25. Is the team equipped with available and reliable
resources?
<--- Score

26. Is the improvement team aware of the different
versions of a process: what they think it is vs. what it
actually is vs. what it should be vs. what it could be?
<--- Score

27. How do you manage unclear Dispute Resolution
requirements?
<--- Score

28. What scope to assess?
<--- Score

29. How do you gather the stories?
<--- Score

30. How often are the team meetings?
<--- Score

31. How did the Dispute Resolution manager receive

input to the development of a Dispute Resolution improvement plan and the estimated completion dates/times of each activity?
<--- Score

32. Is special Dispute Resolution user knowledge required?
<--- Score

33. Does the team have regular meetings?
<--- Score

34. Is Dispute Resolution linked to key stakeholder goals and objectives?
<--- Score

35. What baselines are required to be defined and managed?
<--- Score

36. Are accountability and ownership for Dispute Resolution clearly defined?
<--- Score

37. What are the tasks and definitions?
<--- Score

38. What is the scope of the Dispute Resolution effort?
<--- Score

39. Has/have the customer(s) been identified?
<--- Score

40. What is in the scope and what is not in scope?
<--- Score

41. Is there a completed, verified, and validated high-level 'as is' (not 'should be' or 'could be') stakeholder process map?
<--- Score

42. What are the boundaries of the scope? What is in bounds and what is not? What is the start point? What is the stop point?
<--- Score

43. Who defines (or who defined) the rules and roles?
<--- Score

44. Are customer(s) identified and segmented according to their different needs and requirements?
<--- Score

45. What key stakeholder process output measure(s) does Dispute Resolution leverage and how?
<--- Score

46. What is out of scope?
<--- Score

47. Have the customer needs been translated into specific, measurable requirements? How?
<--- Score

48. Are resources adequate for the scope?
<--- Score

49. What are the core elements of the Dispute Resolution business case?
<--- Score

50. Are roles and responsibilities formally defined?

<--- Score

51. Are stakeholder processes mapped?
<--- Score

52. What system do you use for gathering Dispute Resolution information?
<--- Score

53. What is the definition of Dispute Resolution excellence?
<--- Score

54. Is scope creep really all bad news?
<--- Score

55. Do you all define Dispute Resolution in the same way?
<--- Score

56. What is the worst case scenario?
<--- Score

57. Has the improvement team collected the 'voice of the customer' (obtained feedback – qualitative and quantitative)?
<--- Score

58. Is the team formed and are team leaders (Coaches and Management Leads) assigned?
<--- Score

59. Is the team adequately staffed with the desired cross-functionality? If not, what additional resources are available to the team?
<--- Score

60. What customer feedback methods were used to solicit their input?
<--- Score

61. When is/was the Dispute Resolution start date?
<--- Score

62. How was the 'as is' process map developed, reviewed, verified and validated?
<--- Score

63. How do you manage scope?
<--- Score

64. Are improvement team members fully trained on Dispute Resolution?
<--- Score

65. Are approval levels defined for contracts and supplements to contracts?
<--- Score

66. Will team members regularly document their Dispute Resolution work?
<--- Score

67. Have all basic functions of Dispute Resolution been defined?
<--- Score

68. Have all of the relationships been defined properly?
<--- Score

69. How do you manage changes in Dispute

Resolution requirements?
<--- Score

70. What are the Dispute Resolution use cases?
<--- Score

71. Is there a Dispute Resolution management charter, including stakeholder case, problem and goal statements, scope, milestones, roles and responsibilities, communication plan?
<--- Score

72. What is the scope of Dispute Resolution?
<--- Score

73. Is Dispute Resolution currently on schedule according to the plan?
<--- Score

74. What information should you gather?
<--- Score

75. Is the Dispute Resolution scope complete and appropriately sized?
<--- Score

76. Is there a critical path to deliver Dispute Resolution results?
<--- Score

77. Is full participation by members in regularly held team meetings guaranteed?
<--- Score

78. Who is gathering Dispute Resolution information?
<--- Score

79. How will variation in the actual durations of each activity be dealt with to ensure that the expected Dispute Resolution results are met?
<--- Score

80. Where can you gather more information?
<--- Score

81. Are there any constraints known that bear on the ability to perform Dispute Resolution work? How is the team addressing them?
<--- Score

82. How will the Dispute Resolution team and the group measure complete success of Dispute Resolution?
<--- Score

83. Who is gathering information?
<--- Score

84. How do you keep key subject matter experts in the loop?
<--- Score

85. Has the Dispute Resolution work been fairly and/or equitably divided and delegated among team members who are qualified and capable to perform the work? Has everyone contributed?
<--- Score

86. How do you catch Dispute Resolution definition inconsistencies?
<--- Score

87. Has a project plan, Gantt chart, or similar been developed/completed?
<--- Score

88. How do you gather Dispute Resolution requirements?
<--- Score

89. What sources do you use to gather information for a Dispute Resolution study?
<--- Score

90. What is out-of-scope initially?
<--- Score

91. Has a Dispute Resolution requirement not been met?
<--- Score

92. Is it clearly defined in and to your organization what you do?
<--- Score

93. What intelligence can you gather?
<--- Score

94. What are the rough order estimates on cost savings/opportunities that Dispute Resolution brings?
<--- Score

95. How have you defined all Dispute Resolution requirements first?
<--- Score

96. In what way can you redefine the criteria of choice clients have in your category in your favor?

<--- Score

97. Is the team sponsored by a champion or stakeholder leader?
<--- Score

98. Is data collected and displayed to better understand customer(s) critical needs and requirements.
<--- Score

99. Are required metrics defined, what are they?
<--- Score

100. How do you think the partners involved in Dispute Resolution would have defined success?
<--- Score

101. What is the definition of success?
<--- Score

102. Will a Dispute Resolution production readiness review be required?
<--- Score

103. What scope do you want your strategy to cover?
<--- Score

104. How do you gather requirements?
<--- Score

105. Has a high-level 'as is' process map been completed, verified and validated?
<--- Score

106. Are customers identified and high impact areas

defined?
<--- Score

107. Are task requirements clearly defined?
<--- Score

108. How do you hand over Dispute Resolution context?
<--- Score

109. What happens if Dispute Resolution's scope changes?
<--- Score

110. What would be the goal or target for a Dispute Resolution's improvement team?
<--- Score

111. What is the context?
<--- Score

112. Who are the Dispute Resolution improvement team members, including Management Leads and Coaches?
<--- Score

113. What are the dynamics of the communication plan?
<--- Score

114. How would you define Dispute Resolution leadership?
<--- Score

115. What is in scope?
<--- Score

116. How does the Dispute Resolution manager ensure against scope creep?
<--- Score

117. When is the estimated completion date?
<--- Score

118. Do the problem and goal statements meet the SMART criteria (specific, measurable, attainable, relevant, and time-bound)?
<--- Score

119. What specifically is the problem? Where does it occur? When does it occur? What is its extent?
<--- Score

120. When are meeting minutes sent out? Who is on the distribution list?
<--- Score

121. What are the Dispute Resolution tasks and definitions?
<--- Score

122. Does the scope remain the same?
<--- Score

123. Has the direction changed at all during the course of Dispute Resolution? If so, when did it change and why?
<--- Score

124. What are the Roles and Responsibilities for each team member and its leadership? Where is this documented?

<--- Score

125. Is there regularly 100% attendance at the team meetings? If not, have appointed substitutes attended to preserve cross-functionality and full representation?
<--- Score

126. Are different versions of process maps needed to account for the different types of inputs?
<--- Score

127. How would you define the culture at your organization, how susceptible is it to Dispute Resolution changes?
<--- Score

128. What constraints exist that might impact the team?
<--- Score

129. Is the Dispute Resolution scope manageable?
<--- Score

130. How and when will the baselines be defined?
<--- Score

131. Is there any additional Dispute Resolution definition of success?
<--- Score

132. What are the record-keeping requirements of Dispute Resolution activities?
<--- Score

133. Will team members perform Dispute Resolution

work when assigned and in a timely fashion?
<--- Score

134. Are there different segments of customers?
<--- Score

135. What defines best in class?
<--- Score

136. What Dispute Resolution services do you require?
<--- Score

137. What was the context?
<--- Score

138. What information do you gather?
<--- Score

139. Are team charters developed?
<--- Score

Add up total points for this section:
_ _ _ _ _ = Total points for this section

Divided by: _ _ _ _ _ _ (number of
statements answered) = _ _ _ _ _ _
Average score for this section

Transfer your score to the Dispute
Resolution Index at the beginning of
the Self-Assessment.

CRITERION #3: MEASURE:

INTENT: Gather the correct data.
Measure the current performance and
evolution of the situation.

In my belief, the answer to this
question is clearly defined:

5 Strongly Agree

4 Agree

3 Neutral

2 Disagree

1 Strongly Disagree

1. What relevant entities could be measured?
<--- Score

2. What are the costs of reform?
<--- Score

3. Have you found any 'ground fruit' or 'low-hanging fruit' for immediate remedies to the gap in performance?

<--- Score

4. Can you do Dispute Resolution without complex (expensive) analysis?
<--- Score

5. What is your Dispute Resolution quality cost segregation study?
<--- Score

6. What does your operating model cost?
<--- Score

7. How sensitive must the Dispute Resolution strategy be to cost?
<--- Score

8. How do you aggregate measures across priorities?
<--- Score

9. Which measures and indicators matter?
<--- Score

10. What causes mismanagement?
<--- Score

11. Are you aware of what could cause a problem?
<--- Score

12. Did you tackle the cause or the symptom?
<--- Score

13. Do you verify that corrective actions were taken?
<--- Score

14. What are your customers expectations and

measures?
<--- Score

15. What is the total fixed cost?
<--- Score

16. Is Process Variation Displayed/Communicated?
<--- Score

17. Are losses documented, analyzed, and remedial processes developed to prevent future losses?
<--- Score

18. How do you verify performance?
<--- Score

19. How do you focus on what is right -not who is right?
<--- Score

20. Can you measure the return on analysis?
<--- Score

21. What particular quality tools did the team find helpful in establishing measurements?
<--- Score

22. How do you stay flexible and focused to recognize larger Dispute Resolution results?
<--- Score

23. Where is it measured?
<--- Score

24. What are the agreed upon definitions of the high impact areas, defect(s), unit(s), and opportunities that

will figure into the process capability metrics?
<--- Score

25. How will you measure success?
<--- Score

26. What measurements are possible, practicable and meaningful?
<--- Score

27. What potential environmental factors impact the Dispute Resolution effort?
<--- Score

28. What is the right balance of time and resources between investigation, analysis, and discussion and dissemination?
<--- Score

29. Are supply costs steady or fluctuating?
<--- Score

30. Have the concerns of stakeholders to help identify and define potential barriers been obtained and analyzed?
<--- Score

31. What are allowable costs?
<--- Score

32. What are you verifying?
<--- Score

33. What does verifying compliance entail?
<--- Score

34. When should you bother with diagrams?
<--- Score

35. Which costs should be taken into account?
<--- Score

36. How is progress measured?
<--- Score

37. What tests verify requirements?
<--- Score

38. Will Dispute Resolution have an impact on current business continuity, disaster recovery processes and/ or infrastructure?
<--- Score

39. How do you verify the authenticity of the data and information used?
<--- Score

40. At what cost?
<--- Score

41. Why do you expend time and effort to implement measurement, for whom?
<--- Score

42. What are the Dispute Resolution key cost drivers?
<--- Score

43. Do you effectively measure and reward individual and team performance?
<--- Score

44. How large is the gap between current

performance and the customer-specified (goal) performance?

<--- Score

45. How do you prevent mis-estimating cost?

<--- Score

46. How can you manage cost down?

<--- Score

47. Are you taking your company in the direction of better and revenue or cheaper and cost?

<--- Score

48. How do your measurements capture actionable Dispute Resolution information for use in exceeding your customers expectations and securing your customers engagement?

<--- Score

49. Are the Dispute Resolution benefits worth its costs?

<--- Score

50. How do you measure success?

<--- Score

51. How are you verifying it?

<--- Score

52. Which stakeholder characteristics are analyzed?

<--- Score

53. Have all non-recommended alternatives been analyzed in sufficient detail?

<--- Score

54. How will your organization measure success?
<--- Score

55. When are costs are incurred?
<--- Score

56. How do you do risk analysis of rare, cascading, catastrophic events?
<--- Score

57. What could cause you to change course?
<--- Score

58. Is the scope of Dispute Resolution cost analysis cost-effective?
<--- Score

59. Have the types of risks that may impact Dispute Resolution been identified and analyzed?
<--- Score

60. Is it possible to estimate the impact of unanticipated complexity such as wrong or failed assumptions, feedback, etcetera on proposed reforms?
<--- Score

61. Is data collected on key measures that were identified?
<--- Score

62. What are your operating costs?
<--- Score

63. What are the costs of delaying Dispute Resolution

action?

<--- Score

64. What measurements are being captured?

<--- Score

65. How frequently do you verify your Dispute Resolution strategy?

<--- Score

66. Are you able to realize any cost savings?

<--- Score

67. What causes investor action?

<--- Score

68. What is the cost of rework?

<--- Score

69. Where can you go to verify the info?

<--- Score

70. How frequently do you track Dispute Resolution measures?

<--- Score

71. What are your primary costs, revenues, assets?

<--- Score

72. How do you control the overall costs of your work processes?

<--- Score

73. Has a cost center been established?

<--- Score

74. What is your cost benefit analysis?
<--- Score

75. What are the key input variables? What are the key process variables? What are the key output variables?
<--- Score

76. What are the types and number of measures to use?
<--- Score

77. How will effects be measured?
<--- Score

78. Was a business case (cost/benefit) developed?
<--- Score

79. Is key measure data collection planned and executed, process variation displayed and communicated and performance baselined?
<--- Score

80. How will costs be allocated?
<--- Score

81. Have changes been properly/adequately analyzed for effect?
<--- Score

82. How will you measure your Dispute Resolution effectiveness?
<--- Score

83. Are the units of measure consistent?
<--- Score

84. What are the current costs of the Dispute
Resolution process?
<--- Score

85. What do people want to verify?
<--- Score

86. How do you verify the Dispute Resolution
requirements quality?
<--- Score

87. How do you quantify and qualify impacts?
<--- Score

88. When is Root Cause Analysis Required?
<--- Score

89. Are process variation components displayed/
communicated using suitable charts, graphs, plots?
<--- Score

90. Is the solution cost-effective?
<--- Score

91. Are the measurements objective?
<--- Score

92. Do staff have the necessary skills to collect,
analyze, and report data?
<--- Score

93. Is the cost worth the Dispute Resolution effort ?
<--- Score

94. How is the value delivered by Dispute Resolution
being measured?

<--- Score

95. Are key measures identified and agreed upon?
<--- Score

96. How can you measure Dispute Resolution in a systematic way?
<--- Score

97. What key measures identified indicate the performance of the stakeholder process?
<--- Score

98. Who participated in the data collection for measurements?
<--- Score

99. Who should receive measurement reports?
<--- Score

100. What causes innovation to fail or succeed in your organization?
<--- Score

101. What drives O&M cost?
<--- Score

102. Does a Dispute Resolution quantification method exist?
<--- Score

103. Are there measurements based on task performance?
<--- Score

104. How can a Dispute Resolution test verify your

ideas or assumptions?
<--- Score

105. Are there any easy-to-implement alternatives to Dispute Resolution? Sometimes other solutions are available that do not require the cost implications of a full-blown project?
<--- Score

106. What has the team done to assure the stability and accuracy of the measurement process?
<--- Score

107. Who is involved in verifying compliance?
<--- Score

108. When a disaster occurs, who gets priority?
<--- Score

109. Does the Dispute Resolution task fit the client's priorities?
<--- Score

110. How do you measure lifecycle phases?
<--- Score

111. What are your key Dispute Resolution organizational performance measures, including key short and longer-term financial measures?
<--- Score

112. How to cause the change?
<--- Score

113. How do you identify and analyze stakeholders and their interests?

<--- Score

114. How do you measure efficient delivery of Dispute Resolution services?
<--- Score

115. Is long term and short term variability accounted for?
<--- Score

116. What is the total cost related to deploying Dispute Resolution, including any consulting or professional services?
<--- Score

117. Are there competing Dispute Resolution priorities?
<--- Score

118. What are the operational costs after Dispute Resolution deployment?
<--- Score

119. What are your key Dispute Resolution indicators that you will measure, analyze and track?
<--- Score

120. What charts has the team used to display the components of variation in the process?
<--- Score

121. What are the estimated costs of proposed changes?
<--- Score

122. What is an unallowable cost?

<--- Score

123. Was a life-cycle cost analysis performed?
<--- Score

124. Are missed Dispute Resolution opportunities costing your organization money?
<--- Score

125. Is there an opportunity to verify requirements?
<--- Score

126. Has a cost benefit analysis been performed?
<--- Score

127. How do you know that any Dispute Resolution analysis is complete and comprehensive?
<--- Score

128. What kind of analytics data will be gathered?
<--- Score

129. What happens if cost savings do not materialize?
<--- Score

130. How can you reduce the costs of obtaining inputs?
<--- Score

131. What would it cost to replace your technology?
<--- Score

132. Have you included everything in your Dispute Resolution cost models?
<--- Score

133. Was a data collection plan established?
<--- Score

134. Are high impact defects defined and identified in the stakeholder process?
<--- Score

135. Is a follow-up focused external Dispute Resolution review required?
<--- Score

136. What evidence is there and what is measured?
<--- Score

137. Among the Dispute Resolution product and service cost to be estimated, which is considered hardest to estimate?
<--- Score

138. Is a solid data collection plan established that includes measurement systems analysis?
<--- Score

139. How will success or failure be measured?
<--- Score

140. Do you have any cost Dispute Resolution limitation requirements?
<--- Score

141. How much does it cost?
<--- Score

142. What methods are feasible and acceptable to estimate the impact of reforms?
<--- Score

143. Is there a Performance Baseline?
<--- Score

144. What harm might be caused?
<--- Score

145. How do you verify and develop ideas and innovations?
<--- Score

146. How do you verify and validate the Dispute Resolution data?
<--- Score

147. What are the costs and benefits?
<--- Score

148. How are costs allocated?
<--- Score

149. Does Dispute Resolution analysis isolate the fundamental causes of problems?
<--- Score

150. What are the uncertainties surrounding estimates of impact?
<--- Score

151. What does a Test Case verify?
<--- Score

152. Do the benefits outweigh the costs?
<--- Score

153. How does cost-to-serve analysis help?

<--- Score

154. What is measured? Why?
<--- Score

155. Does Dispute Resolution systematically track and analyze outcomes for accountability and quality improvement?
<--- Score

156. Does your organization systematically track and analyze outcomes related for accountability and quality improvement?
<--- Score

157. Do you aggressively reward and promote the people who have the biggest impact on creating excellent Dispute Resolution services/products?
<--- Score

158. Is data collection planned and executed?
<--- Score

159. The approach of traditional Dispute Resolution works for detail complexity but is focused on a systematic approach rather than an understanding of the nature of systems themselves, what approach will permit your organization to deal with the kind of unpredictable emergent behaviors that dynamic complexity can introduce?
<--- Score

160. How will measures be used to manage and adapt?
<--- Score

161. Does Dispute Resolution analysis show the relationships among important Dispute Resolution factors?
<--- Score

162. How do you verify if Dispute Resolution is built right?
<--- Score

163. What would be a real cause for concern?
<--- Score

164. How do you measure variability?
<--- Score

165. What does losing customers cost your organization?
<--- Score

166. How do you verify Dispute Resolution completeness and accuracy?
<--- Score

167. What could cause delays in the schedule?
<--- Score

168. What causes extra work or rework?
<--- Score

169. What do you measure and why?
<--- Score

170. How do you verify your resources?
<--- Score

171. What disadvantage does this cause for the user?

<--- Score

172. What can be used to verify compliance?
<--- Score

173. How can you measure the performance?
<--- Score

174. Why do the measurements/indicators matter?
<--- Score

175. What data was collected (past, present, future/ongoing)?
<--- Score

176. How are measurements made?
<--- Score

177. How is performance measured?
<--- Score

178. Are actual costs in line with budgeted costs?
<--- Score

179. Have design-to-cost goals been established?
<--- Score

180. Do you have a flow diagram of what happens?
<--- Score

181. What is your decision requirements diagram?
<--- Score

182. How can you reduce costs?
<--- Score

183. Have you made assumptions about the shape of the future, particularly its impact on your customers and competitors?
<--- Score

184. Are indirect costs charged to the Dispute Resolution program?
<--- Score

Add up total points for this section:
_ _ _ _ _ = Total points for this section

Divided by: _ _ _ _ _ _ (number of statements answered) = _ _ _ _ _ _
Average score for this section

Transfer your score to the Dispute Resolution Index at the beginning of the Self-Assessment.

CRITERION #4: ANALYZE:

INTENT: Analyze causes, assumptions and hypotheses.

In my belief, the answer to this question is clearly defined:

5 Strongly Agree

4 Agree

3 Neutral

2 Disagree

1 Strongly Disagree

1. What tools were used to narrow the list of possible causes?
<--- Score

2. Do your employees have the opportunity to do what they do best everyday?
<--- Score

3. What are the best opportunities for value improvement?

<--- Score

4. How do mission and objectives affect the Dispute Resolution processes of your organization?
<--- Score

5. What qualifications are necessary?
<--- Score

6. What data do you need to collect?
<--- Score

7. Is the required Dispute Resolution data gathered?
<--- Score

8. Are your outputs consistent?
<--- Score

9. Is pre-qualification of suppliers carried out?
<--- Score

10. What controls do you have in place to protect data?
<--- Score

11. What are your current levels and trends in key measures or indicators of Dispute Resolution product and process performance that are important to and directly serve your customers? How do these results compare with the performance of your competitors and other organizations with similar offerings?
<--- Score

12. Are all staff in core Dispute Resolution subjects Highly Qualified?
<--- Score

13. What is the process of chargeback and dispute resolution?
<--- Score

14. Should you invest in industry-recognized qualifications?
<--- Score

15. Who qualifies to gain access to data?
<--- Score

16. Where is the data coming from to measure compliance?
<--- Score

17. What is your organizations system for selecting qualified vendors?
<--- Score

18. What kind of crime could a potential new hire have committed that would not only not disqualify him/her from being hired by your organization, but would actually indicate that he/she might be a particularly good fit?
<--- Score

19. What tools were used to generate the list of possible causes?
<--- Score

20. How does the organization define, manage, and improve its Dispute Resolution processes?
<--- Score

21. An organizationally feasible system request is one

that considers the mission, goals and objectives of the organization, key questions are: is the Dispute Resolution solution request practical and will it solve a problem or take advantage of an opportunity to achieve company goals?
<--- Score

22. Think about the functions involved in your Dispute Resolution project, what processes flow from these functions?
<--- Score

23. What are evaluation criteria for the output?
<--- Score

24. How often will data be collected for measures?
<--- Score

25. What other jobs or tasks affect the performance of the steps in the Dispute Resolution process?
<--- Score

26. Were Pareto charts (or similar) used to portray the 'heavy hitters' (or key sources of variation)?
<--- Score

27. How do you define collaboration and team output?
<--- Score

28. Have you defined which data is gathered how?
<--- Score

29. Were there any improvement opportunities identified from the process analysis?
<--- Score

30. What are your best practices for minimizing Dispute Resolution project risk, while demonstrating incremental value and quick wins throughout the Dispute Resolution project lifecycle?
<--- Score

31. What are your Dispute Resolution processes?
<--- Score

32. What are the revised rough estimates of the financial savings/opportunity for Dispute Resolution improvements?
<--- Score

33. Where is Dispute Resolution data gathered?
<--- Score

34. What is the complexity of the output produced?
<--- Score

35. Is the suppliers process defined and controlled?
<--- Score

36. Who will gather what data?
<--- Score

37. What information qualified as important?
<--- Score

38. A compounding model resolution with available relevant data can often provide insight towards a solution methodology; which Dispute Resolution models, tools and techniques are necessary?
<--- Score

39. What are your key performance measures or indicators and in-process measures for the control and improvement of your Dispute Resolution processes?
<--- Score

40. Who gets your output?
<--- Score

41. Have the problem and goal statements been updated to reflect the additional knowledge gained from the analyze phase?
<--- Score

42. What training and qualifications will you need?
<--- Score

43. How do your work systems and key work processes relate to and capitalize on your core competencies?
<--- Score

44. Are all team members qualified for all tasks?
<--- Score

45. What were the financial benefits resulting from any 'ground fruit or low-hanging fruit' (quick fixes)?
<--- Score

46. Have any additional benefits been identified that will result from closing all or most of the gaps?
<--- Score

47. What are the disruptive Dispute Resolution technologies that enable your organization to radically change your business processes?

<--- Score

48. Did any value-added analysis or 'lean thinking'
take place to identify some of the gaps shown on the
'as is' process map?
<--- Score

49. What quality tools were used to get through the
analyze phase?
<--- Score

50. Do you have the authority to produce the output?
<--- Score

51. How do you use Dispute Resolution data and
information to support organizational decision
making and innovation?
<--- Score

52. What are your current levels and trends in key
Dispute Resolution measures or indicators of product
and process performance that are important to and
directly serve your customers?
<--- Score

53. Identify an operational issue in your organization,
for example, could a particular task be done more
quickly or more efficiently by Dispute Resolution?
<--- Score

54. What successful thing are you doing today that
may be blinding you to new growth opportunities?
<--- Score

55. Do your contracts/agreements contain data
security obligations?

<--- Score

56. What is the Value Stream Mapping?
<--- Score

57. Record-keeping requirements flow from the records needed as inputs, outputs, controls and for transformation of a Dispute Resolution process, are the records needed as inputs to the Dispute Resolution process available?
<--- Score

58. How do you identify specific Dispute Resolution investment opportunities and emerging trends?
<--- Score

59. What is your dispute resolution process?
<--- Score

60. What methods do you use to gather Dispute Resolution data?
<--- Score

61. What did the team gain from developing a sub-process map?
<--- Score

62. How is the way you as the leader think and process information affecting your organizational culture?
<--- Score

63. Who is involved with workflow mapping?
<--- Score

64. Has data output been validated?
<--- Score

65. Do staff qualifications match your project?
<--- Score

66. How are outputs preserved and protected?
<--- Score

67. Is the Dispute Resolution process severely broken such that a re-design is necessary?
<--- Score

68. Were any designed experiments used to generate additional insight into the data analysis?
<--- Score

69. Did any additional data need to be collected?
<--- Score

70. What is your organizations process which leads to recognition of value generation?
<--- Score

71. Is data and process analysis, root cause analysis and quantifying the gap/opportunity in place?
<--- Score

72. Was a detailed process map created to amplify critical steps of the 'as is' stakeholder process?
<--- Score

73. What were the crucial 'moments of truth' on the process map?
<--- Score

74. Is the gap/opportunity displayed and communicated in financial terms?

<--- Score

75. What are the necessary qualifications?
<--- Score

76. How do you measure the operational performance of your key work systems and processes, including productivity, cycle time, and other appropriate measures of process effectiveness, efficiency, and innovation?
<--- Score

77. How difficult is it to qualify what Dispute Resolution ROI is?
<--- Score

78. How has the Dispute Resolution data been gathered?
<--- Score

79. What qualifies as competition?
<--- Score

80. What other organizational variables, such as reward systems or communication systems, affect the performance of this Dispute Resolution process?
<--- Score

81. What qualifications are needed?
<--- Score

82. What do you need to qualify?
<--- Score

83. How is Dispute Resolution data gathered?
<--- Score

84. What does the data say about the performance of the stakeholder process?
<--- Score

85. What will drive Dispute Resolution change?
<--- Score

86. How was the detailed process map generated, verified, and validated?
<--- Score

87. Is the performance gap determined?
<--- Score

88. Do you have a review process (to determine steering committee effectiveness) and a process for dispute resolution?
<--- Score

89. Are Dispute Resolution changes recognized early enough to be approved through the regular process?
<--- Score

90. How many input/output points does it require?
<--- Score

91. What Dispute Resolution metrics are outputs of the process?
<--- Score

92. What qualifications and skills do you need?
<--- Score

93. Has an output goal been set?
<--- Score

94. What Dispute Resolution data do you gather or use now?
<--- Score

95. Think about some of the processes you undertake within your organization, which do you own?
<--- Score

96. What data is gathered?
<--- Score

97. Is the final output clearly identified?
<--- Score

98. How do you implement and manage your work processes to ensure that they meet design requirements?
<--- Score

99. Can you add value to the current Dispute Resolution decision-making process (largely qualitative) by incorporating uncertainty modeling (more quantitative)?
<--- Score

100. Where can you get qualified talent today?
<--- Score

101. How do you promote understanding that opportunity for improvement is not criticism of the status quo, or the people who created the status quo?
<--- Score

102. What are the personnel training and qualifications required?

<--- Score

103. Do you, as a leader, bounce back quickly from setbacks?
<--- Score

104. What conclusions were drawn from the team's data collection and analysis? How did the team reach these conclusions?
<--- Score

105. What resources go in to get the desired output?
<--- Score

106. Was a cause-and-effect diagram used to explore the different types of causes (or sources of variation)?
<--- Score

107. What are your outputs?
<--- Score

108. What qualifications do Dispute Resolution leaders need?
<--- Score

109. Are gaps between current performance and the goal performance identified?
<--- Score

110. What is the cost of poor quality as supported by the team's analysis?
<--- Score

111. What process should you select for improvement?
<--- Score

112. How is the data gathered?
<--- Score

113. Do your leaders quickly bounce back from setbacks?
<--- Score

114. What output to create?
<--- Score

115. Do several people in different organizational units assist with the Dispute Resolution process?
<--- Score

116. What is the output?
<--- Score

117. How is the Dispute Resolution Value Stream Mapping managed?
<--- Score

Add up total points for this section:
_____ = Total points for this section

Divided by: _____ (number of statements answered) = _____
Average score for this section

Transfer your score to the Dispute Resolution Index at the beginning of the Self-Assessment.

CRITERION #5: IMPROVE:

INTENT: Develop a practical solution.
Innovate, establish and test the
solution and to measure the results.

In my belief, the answer to this
question is clearly defined:

5 Strongly Agree

4 Agree

3 Neutral

2 Disagree

1 Strongly Disagree

1. How do you measure improved Dispute Resolution
service perception, and satisfaction?
<--- Score

2. Which of the recognised risks out of all risks can be
most likely transferred?
<--- Score

3. Are you assessing Dispute Resolution and risk?

<--- Score

4. Do you combine technical expertise with business knowledge and Dispute Resolution Key topics include lifecycles, development approaches, requirements and how to make a business case?
<--- Score

5. How do you link measurement and risk?
<--- Score

6. Who will be responsible for making the decisions to include or exclude requested changes once Dispute Resolution is underway?
<--- Score

7. Are risk triggers captured?
<--- Score

8. How do the Dispute Resolution results compare with the performance of your competitors and other organizations with similar offerings?
<--- Score

9. Is the implementation plan designed?
<--- Score

10. What improvements have been achieved?
<--- Score

11. What tools were used to tap into the creativity and encourage 'outside the box' thinking?
<--- Score

12. How did the team generate the list of possible solutions?

<--- Score

13. What to do with the results or outcomes of measurements?
<--- Score

14. Is there a high likelihood that any recommendations will achieve their intended results?
<--- Score

15. For decision problems, how do you develop a decision statement?
<--- Score

16. Who will be using the results of the measurement activities?
<--- Score

17. How do you go about comparing Dispute Resolution approaches/solutions?
<--- Score

18. How will you measure the results?
<--- Score

19. For estimation problems, how do you develop an estimation statement?
<--- Score

20. How can skill-level changes improve Dispute Resolution?
<--- Score

21. Is the optimal solution selected based on testing and analysis?
<--- Score

22. How do you evaluate its success?
<--- Score

23. What are your current levels and trends in key measures or indicators of workforce and leader development?
<--- Score

24. How significant is the improvement in the eyes of the end user?
<--- Score

25. What is the Dispute Resolution's sustainability risk?
<--- Score

26. What lessons, if any, from a pilot were incorporated into the design of the full-scale solution?
<--- Score

27. What is the implementation plan?
<--- Score

28. Can the solution be designed and implemented within an acceptable time period?
<--- Score

29. How do you keep improving Dispute Resolution?
<--- Score

30. How will the team or the process owner(s) monitor the implementation plan to see that it is working as intended?
<--- Score

31. What attendant changes will need to be made to

ensure that the solution is successful?
<--- Score

32. Does the goal represent a desired result that can be measured?
<--- Score

33. Where can an employee go for further information about the dispute resolution program?
<--- Score

34. How do you improve productivity?
<--- Score

35. What internal dispute resolution mechanisms are available?
<--- Score

36. How will you know that a change is an improvement?
<--- Score

37. What actually has to improve and by how much?
<--- Score

38. What error proofing will be done to address some of the discrepancies observed in the 'as is' process?
<--- Score

39. Who controls the risk?
<--- Score

40. Who are the people involved in developing and implementing Dispute Resolution?
<--- Score

41. What is Dispute Resolution's impact on utilizing the best solution(s)?
<--- Score

42. How risky is your organization?
<--- Score

43. Describe the design of the pilot and what tests were conducted, if any?
<--- Score

44. How do you improve your likelihood of success ?
<--- Score

45. Is there a small-scale pilot for proposed improvement(s)? What conclusions were drawn from the outcomes of a pilot?
<--- Score

46. Do you cover the five essential competencies: Communication, Collaboration,Innovation, Adaptability, and Leadership that improve an organizations ability to leverage the new Dispute Resolution in a volatile global economy?
<--- Score

47. Is Dispute Resolution covered in the Master Service Agreement?
<--- Score

48. Are new and improved process ('should be') maps developed?
<--- Score

49. When you map the key players in your own work

and the types/domains of relationships with them, which relationships do you find easy and which challenging, and why?
<--- Score

50. Are there any constraints (technical, political, cultural, or otherwise) that would inhibit certain solutions?
<--- Score

51. Explorations of the frontiers of Dispute Resolution will help you build influence, improve Dispute Resolution, optimize decision making, and sustain change, what is your approach?
<--- Score

52. What is the team's contingency plan for potential problems occurring in implementation?
<--- Score

53. Are improved process ('should be') maps modified based on pilot data and analysis?
<--- Score

54. How will the group know that the solution worked?
<--- Score

55. Who do you report Dispute Resolution results to?
<--- Score

56. What is the magnitude of the improvements?
<--- Score

57. What are the implications of the one critical Dispute Resolution decision 10 minutes, 10 months,

and 10 years from now?
<--- Score

58. Who controls key decisions that will be made?
<--- Score

59. What issues should be considered when deciding on a dispute resolution method?
<--- Score

60. How can you improve performance?
<--- Score

61. How are policy decisions made and where?
<--- Score

62. What is the risk?
<--- Score

63. What communications are necessary to support the implementation of the solution?
<--- Score

64. Is a solution implementation plan established, including schedule/work breakdown structure, resources, risk management plan, cost/budget, and control plan?
<--- Score

65. What do you want to improve?
<--- Score

66. How do you define the solutions' scope?
<--- Score

67. How does the solution remove the key sources of

issues discovered in the analyze phase?
<--- Score

68. How will you know that you have improved?
<--- Score

69. Who makes the Dispute Resolution decisions in your organization?
<--- Score

70. In the past few months, what is the smallest change you have made that has had the biggest positive result? What was it about that small change that produced the large return?
<--- Score

71. What can you do to improve?
<--- Score

72. What were the underlying assumptions on the cost-benefit analysis?
<--- Score

73. What needs improvement? Why?
<--- Score

74. The dispute resolution provision: the most important contractual provision?
<--- Score

75. What practices helps your organization to develop its capacity to recognize patterns?
<--- Score

76. Does a good decision guarantee a good outcome?
<--- Score

77. Are possible solutions generated and tested?
<--- Score

78. What does the 'should be' process map/design look like?
<--- Score

79. If you could go back in time five years, what decision would you make differently? What is your best guess as to what decision you're making today you might regret five years from now?
<--- Score

80. How do you manage and improve your Dispute Resolution work systems to deliver customer value and achieve organizational success and sustainability?
<--- Score

81. How does the team improve its work?
<--- Score

82. Is there a cost/benefit analysis of optimal solution(s)?
<--- Score

83. Was a Dispute Resolution charter developed?
<--- Score

84. How do you measure progress and evaluate training effectiveness?
<--- Score

85. Was a pilot designed for the proposed solution(s)?
<--- Score

86. To what extent does management recognize Dispute Resolution as a tool to increase the results?
<--- Score

87. Risk Identification: What are the possible risk events your organization faces in relation to Dispute Resolution?
<--- Score

88. Will the controls trigger any other risks?
<--- Score

89. Risk factors: what are the characteristics of Dispute Resolution that make it risky?
<--- Score

90. How will you know when its improved?
<--- Score

91. Is a contingency plan established?
<--- Score

92. How do you improve Dispute Resolution service perception, and satisfaction?
<--- Score

93. Is the solution technically practical?
<--- Score

94. Is pilot data collected and analyzed?
<--- Score

95. Is the scope clearly documented?
<--- Score

96. At what point will vulnerability assessments

be performed once Dispute Resolution is put into production (e.g., ongoing Risk Management after implementation)?
<--- Score

97. Dispute Resolution risk decisions: whose call Is It?
<--- Score

98. How do you decide how much to remunerate an employee?
<--- Score

99. What tools were most useful during the improve phase?
<--- Score

100. Is supporting Dispute Resolution documentation required?
<--- Score

101. Are decisions made in a timely manner?
<--- Score

102. Risk events: what are the things that could go wrong?
<--- Score

103. Do those selected for the Dispute Resolution team have a good general understanding of what Dispute Resolution is all about?
<--- Score

104. Can you identify any significant risks or exposures to Dispute Resolution third- parties (vendors, service providers, alliance partners etc) that concern you?
<--- Score

105. Who will be responsible for documenting the Dispute Resolution requirements in detail?
<--- Score

106. What tools do you use once you have decided on a Dispute Resolution strategy and more importantly how do you choose?
<--- Score

107. Is the measure of success for Dispute Resolution understandable to a variety of people?
<--- Score

108. What resources are required for the improvement efforts?
<--- Score

109. Why improve in the first place?
<--- Score

110. What should a proof of concept or pilot accomplish?
<--- Score

111. Have you identified breakpoints and/or risk tolerances that will trigger broad consideration of a potential need for intervention or modification of strategy?
<--- Score

112. Are the best solutions selected?
<--- Score

113. What tools were used to evaluate the potential solutions?

<--- Score

114. Were any criteria developed to assist the team in testing and evaluating potential solutions?
<--- Score

115. How can you improve Dispute Resolution?
<--- Score

116. How do you measure risk?
<--- Score

117. What went well, what should change, what can improve?
<--- Score

Add up total points for this section:
_ _ _ _ _ = Total points for this section

Divided by: _ _ _ _ _ _ (number of statements answered) = _ _ _ _ _ _
Average score for this section

Transfer your score to the Dispute Resolution Index at the beginning of the Self-Assessment.

CRITERION #6: CONTROL:

INTENT: Implement the practical
solution. Maintain the performance and
correct possible complications.

In my belief, the answer to this
question is clearly defined:

5 Strongly Agree

4 Agree

3 Neutral

2 Disagree

1 Strongly Disagree

1. Does the response plan contain a definite closed
loop continual improvement scheme (e.g., plan-do-
check-act)?
<--- Score

2. What are the key elements of your Dispute
Resolution performance improvement system,
including your evaluation, organizational learning,
and innovation processes?

<--- Score

3. Are there documented procedures?
<--- Score

4. Are operating procedures consistent?
<--- Score

5. Will the team be available to assist members in planning investigations?
<--- Score

6. How likely is the current Dispute Resolution plan to come in on schedule or on budget?
<--- Score

7. Is reporting being used or needed?
<--- Score

8. What do your reports reflect?
<--- Score

9. Does Dispute Resolution appropriately measure and monitor risk?
<--- Score

10. Is the Dispute Resolution test/monitoring cost justified?
<--- Score

11. What should the next improvement project be that is related to Dispute Resolution?
<--- Score

12. Are the planned controls in place?
<--- Score

13. Has the Dispute Resolution value of standards been quantified?
<--- Score

14. Do you monitor the Dispute Resolution decisions made and fine tune them as they evolve?
<--- Score

15. Is knowledge gained on process shared and institutionalized?
<--- Score

16. What is the best design framework for Dispute Resolution organization now that, in a post industrial-age if the top-down, command and control model is no longer relevant?
<--- Score

17. Is there a Dispute Resolution Communication plan covering who needs to get what information when?
<--- Score

18. Who sets the Dispute Resolution standards?
<--- Score

19. Is there a recommended audit plan for routine surveillance inspections of Dispute Resolution's gains?
<--- Score

20. How might the group capture best practices and lessons learned so as to leverage improvements?
<--- Score

21. Is there a transfer of ownership and knowledge to process owner and process team tasked with the

responsibilities.
<--- Score

22. Do the Dispute Resolution decisions you make today help people and the planet tomorrow?
<--- Score

23. What are the known security controls?
<--- Score

24. Are controls in place and consistently applied?
<--- Score

25. How do you establish and deploy modified action plans if circumstances require a shift in plans and rapid execution of new plans?
<--- Score

26. Will existing staff require re-training, for example, to learn new business processes?
<--- Score

27. Against what alternative is success being measured?
<--- Score

28. Does a troubleshooting guide exist or is it needed?
<--- Score

29. How will report readings be checked to effectively monitor performance?
<--- Score

30. What other systems, operations, processes, and infrastructures (hiring practices, staffing, training, incentives/rewards, metrics/dashboards/scorecards,

etc.) need updates, additions, changes, or deletions in order to facilitate knowledge transfer and improvements?
<--- Score

31. Are suggested corrective/restorative actions indicated on the response plan for known causes to problems that might surface?
<--- Score

32. Are new process steps, standards, and documentation ingrained into normal operations?
<--- Score

33. How will new or emerging customer needs/ requirements be checked/communicated to orient the process toward meeting the new specifications and continually reducing variation?
<--- Score

34. How do you plan on providing proper recognition and disclosure of supporting companies?
<--- Score

35. How will Dispute Resolution decisions be made and monitored?
<--- Score

36. Is a response plan in place for when the input, process, or output measures indicate an 'out-of-control' condition?
<--- Score

37. Is there a control plan in place for sustaining improvements (short and long-term)?
<--- Score

38. How can you best use all of your knowledge repositories to enhance learning and sharing?
<--- Score

39. What are the critical parameters to watch?
<--- Score

40. How do you select, collect, align, and integrate Dispute Resolution data and information for tracking daily operations and overall organizational performance, including progress relative to strategic objectives and action plans?
<--- Score

41. What do you stand for--and what are you against?
<--- Score

42. What key inputs and outputs are being measured on an ongoing basis?
<--- Score

43. Can support from partners be adjusted?
<--- Score

44. How do you plan for the cost of succession?
<--- Score

45. How will the process owner and team be able to hold the gains?
<--- Score

46. How widespread is its use?
<--- Score

47. How is Dispute Resolution project cost planned,

managed, monitored?
<--- Score

48. How do controls support value?
<--- Score

49. Does the Dispute Resolution performance meet the customer's requirements?
<--- Score

50. What are you attempting to measure/monitor?
<--- Score

51. How do you monitor usage and cost?
<--- Score

52. Will any special training be provided for results interpretation?
<--- Score

53. How do your controls stack up?
<--- Score

54. In the case of a Dispute Resolution project, the criteria for the audit derive from implementation objectives, an audit of a Dispute Resolution project involves assessing whether the recommendations outlined for implementation have been met, can you track that any Dispute Resolution project is implemented as planned, and is it working?
<--- Score

55. How do senior leaders actions reflect a commitment to the organizations Dispute Resolution values?
<--- Score

56. Is new knowledge gained imbedded in the response plan?
<--- Score

57. Who is going to spread your message?
<--- Score

58. Is there documentation that will support the successful operation of the improvement?
<--- Score

59. Is there an action plan in case of emergencies?
<--- Score

60. How do you encourage people to take control and responsibility?
<--- Score

61. What quality tools were useful in the control phase?
<--- Score

62. Who controls critical resources?
<--- Score

63. Who will be in control?
<--- Score

64. Will your goals reflect your program budget?
<--- Score

65. Are documented procedures clear and easy to follow for the operators?
<--- Score

66. Have new or revised work instructions resulted?
<--- Score

67. What is the recommended frequency of auditing?
<--- Score

68. Is there a documented and implemented monitoring plan?
<--- Score

69. What do you measure to verify effectiveness gains?
<--- Score

70. Are you measuring, monitoring and predicting Dispute Resolution activities to optimize operations and profitability, and enhancing outcomes?
<--- Score

71. Who is the Dispute Resolution process owner?
<--- Score

72. What is your theory of human motivation, and how does your compensation plan fit with that view?
<--- Score

73. How will input, process, and output variables be checked to detect for sub-optimal conditions?
<--- Score

74. What are your results for key measures or indicators of the accomplishment of your Dispute Resolution strategy and action plans, including building and strengthening core competencies?
<--- Score

75. Implementation Planning: is a pilot needed to test the changes before a full roll out occurs?
<--- Score

76. How will you measure your QA plan's effectiveness?
<--- Score

77. What should you measure to verify efficiency gains?
<--- Score

78. Have you developed dispute resolution mechanisms and a game plan for contingencies?
<--- Score

79. What can you control?
<--- Score

80. Is a response plan established and deployed?
<--- Score

81. Does job training on the documented procedures need to be part of the process team's education and training?
<--- Score

82. Are pertinent alerts monitored, analyzed and distributed to appropriate personnel?
<--- Score

83. How will the process owner verify improvement in present and future sigma levels, process capabilities?
<--- Score

84. What is the control/monitoring plan?

<--- Score

85. Who has control over resources?
<--- Score

86. What adjustments to the strategies are needed?
<--- Score

87. Has the improved process and its steps been standardized?
<--- Score

88. How will the day-to-day responsibilities for monitoring and continual improvement be transferred from the improvement team to the process owner?
<--- Score

89. How is change control managed?
<--- Score

90. Is there a standardized process?
<--- Score

91. How do you spread information?
<--- Score

92. Do you monitor the effectiveness of your Dispute Resolution activities?
<--- Score

93. What other areas of the group might benefit from the Dispute Resolution team's improvements, knowledge, and learning?
<--- Score

94. Where do ideas that reach policy makers and planners as proposals for Dispute Resolution strengthening and reform actually originate?
<--- Score

95. Are the planned controls working?
<--- Score

96. You may have created your quality measures at a time when you lacked resources, technology wasn't up to the required standard, or low service levels were the industry norm. Have those circumstances changed?
<--- Score

97. Act/Adjust: What Do you Need to Do Differently?
<--- Score

98. Can you adapt and adjust to changing Dispute Resolution situations?
<--- Score

Add up total points for this section:
_____ = Total points for this section

Divided by: _____ (number of statements answered) = _____
Average score for this section

Transfer your score to the Dispute Resolution Index at the beginning of the Self-Assessment.

CRITERION #7: SUSTAIN:

INTENT: Retain the benefits.

In my belief, the answer to this question is clearly defined:

5 Strongly Agree

4 Agree

3 Neutral

2 Disagree

1 Strongly Disagree

1. Who, on the executive team or the board, has spoken to a customer recently?
<--- Score

2. How will you motivate the stakeholders with the least vested interest?
<--- Score

3. Why not do Dispute Resolution?
<--- Score

4. What is effective Dispute Resolution?
<--- Score

5. Are the criteria for selecting recommendations stated?
<--- Score

6. Which Dispute Resolution goals are the most important?
<--- Score

7. What one word do you want to own in the minds of your customers, employees, and partners?
<--- Score

8. Are you maintaining a past–present–future perspective throughout the Dispute Resolution discussion?
<--- Score

9. What may be the consequences for the performance of an organization if all stakeholders are not consulted regarding Dispute Resolution?
<--- Score

10. How do you deal with Dispute Resolution changes?
<--- Score

11. Why is it important to have senior management support for a Dispute Resolution project?
<--- Score

12. What counts that you are not counting?
<--- Score

13. How do you cross-sell and up-sell your Dispute Resolution success?
<--- Score

14. What would you recommend your friend do if he/she were facing this dilemma?
<--- Score

15. Is the Dispute Resolution organization completing tasks effectively and efficiently?
<--- Score

16. Operational - will it work?
<--- Score

17. Is the impact that Dispute Resolution has shown?
<--- Score

18. How will you know that the Dispute Resolution project has been successful?
<--- Score

19. Is maximizing Dispute Resolution protection the same as minimizing Dispute Resolution loss?
<--- Score

20. What are specific Dispute Resolution rules to follow?
<--- Score

21. How do you ensure that implementations of Dispute Resolution products are done in a way that ensures safety?
<--- Score

22. What are strategies for increasing support and

reducing opposition?
<--- Score

23. What will be the consequences to the stakeholder (financial, reputation etc) if Dispute Resolution does not go ahead or fails to deliver the objectives?
<--- Score

24. How do you foster the skills, knowledge, talents, attributes, and characteristics you want to have?
<--- Score

25. What happens when a new employee joins the organization?
<--- Score

26. What happens at your organization when people fail?
<--- Score

27. What are the essentials of internal Dispute Resolution management?
<--- Score

28. Who do we want your customers to become?
<--- Score

29. Who will be responsible for deciding whether Dispute Resolution goes ahead or not after the initial investigations?
<--- Score

30. What is something you believe that nearly no one agrees with you on?
<--- Score

31. What are the long-term Dispute Resolution goals?
<--- Score

32. What is the overall business strategy?
<--- Score

33. What are the short and long-term Dispute Resolution goals?
<--- Score

34. What would have to be true for the option on the table to be the best possible choice?
<--- Score

35. How do you manage Dispute Resolution Knowledge Management (KM)?
<--- Score

36. How can you negotiate Dispute Resolution successfully with a stubborn boss, an irate client, or a deceitful coworker?
<--- Score

37. Why will customers want to buy your organizations products/services?
<--- Score

38. What is your question? Why?
<--- Score

39. How do you foster innovation?
<--- Score

40. What have you done to protect your business from competitive encroachment?
<--- Score

41. Do you feel that more should be done in the Dispute Resolution area?
<--- Score

42. How do customers see your organization?
<--- Score

43. Did your employees make progress today?
<--- Score

44. What is the craziest thing you can do?
<--- Score

45. What could happen if you do not do it?
<--- Score

46. Are you making progress, and are you making progress as Dispute Resolution leaders?
<--- Score

47. What trouble can you get into?
<--- Score

48. What are the business goals Dispute Resolution is aiming to achieve?
<--- Score

49. Who is the main stakeholder, with ultimate responsibility for driving Dispute Resolution forward?
<--- Score

50. What are you trying to prove to yourself, and how might it be hijacking your life and business success?
<--- Score

51. What are your personal philosophies regarding Dispute Resolution and how do they influence your work?
<--- Score

52. Think of your Dispute Resolution project, what are the main functions?
<--- Score

53. How can you incorporate support to ensure safe and effective use of Dispute Resolution into the services that you provide?
<--- Score

54. Which functions and people interact with the supplier and or customer?
<--- Score

55. Are you changing as fast as the world around you?
<--- Score

56. What current systems have to be understood and/or changed?
<--- Score

57. Are there any activities that you can take off your to do list?
<--- Score

58. What is a feasible sequencing of reform initiatives over time?
<--- Score

59. How do you proactively clarify deliverables and Dispute Resolution quality expectations?
<--- Score

60. How can you become more high-tech but still be high touch?
<--- Score

61. How do you determine the key elements that affect Dispute Resolution workforce satisfaction, how are these elements determined for different workforce groups and segments?
<--- Score

62. Who are the key stakeholders?
<--- Score

63. What you are going to do to affect the numbers?
<--- Score

64. If your customer were your grandmother, would you tell her to buy what you're selling?
<--- Score

65. In a project to restructure Dispute Resolution outcomes, which stakeholders would you involve?
<--- Score

66. Is Dispute Resolution dependent on the successful delivery of a current project?
<--- Score

67. Is your strategy driving your strategy? Or is the way in which you allocate resources driving your strategy?
<--- Score

68. How do you create buy-in?
<--- Score

69. How much does Dispute Resolution help?
<--- Score

70. What are current Dispute Resolution paradigms?
<--- Score

71. What projects are going on in the organization today, and what resources are those projects using from the resource pools?
<--- Score

72. Do Dispute Resolution rules make a reasonable demand on a users capabilities?
<--- Score

73. Do you know who is a friend or a foe?
<--- Score

74. Which models, tools and techniques are necessary?
<--- Score

75. Where can you break convention?
<--- Score

76. What are the top 3 things at the forefront of your Dispute Resolution agendas for the next 3 years?
<--- Score

77. What are the usability implications of Dispute Resolution actions?
<--- Score

78. Were lessons learned captured and communicated?

<--- Score

79. How do you listen to customers to obtain actionable information?
<--- Score

80. Who are four people whose careers you have enhanced?
<--- Score

81. Do you say no to customers for no reason?
<--- Score

82. What goals did you miss?
<--- Score

83. Is there any existing Dispute Resolution governance structure?
<--- Score

84. If you weren't already in this business, would you enter it today? And if not, what are you going to do about it?
<--- Score

85. Marketing budgets are tighter, consumers are more skeptical, and social media has changed forever the way we talk about Dispute Resolution, how do you gain traction?
<--- Score

86. Are you using a design thinking approach and integrating Innovation, Dispute Resolution Experience, and Brand Value?
<--- Score

87. What does your signature ensure?
<--- Score

88. What business benefits will Dispute Resolution goals deliver if achieved?
<--- Score

89. Who do you want your customers to become?
<--- Score

90. What have been your experiences in defining long range Dispute Resolution goals?
<--- Score

91. Who have you, as a company, historically been when you've been at your best?
<--- Score

92. Do you think Dispute Resolution accomplishes the goals you expect it to accomplish?
<--- Score

93. Do you have past Dispute Resolution successes?
<--- Score

94. How long will it take to change?
<--- Score

95. Do you provide for arbitration under the EPC contracts?
<--- Score

96. How likely is it that a customer would recommend your company to a friend or colleague?
<--- Score

97. How much contingency will be available in the budget?
<--- Score

98. How do senior leaders deploy your organizations vision and values through your leadership system, to the workforce, to key suppliers and partners, and to customers and other stakeholders, as appropriate?
<--- Score

99. If your company went out of business tomorrow, would anyone who doesn't get a paycheck here care?
<--- Score

100. Are new benefits received and understood?
<--- Score

101. What must you excel at?
<--- Score

102. How do you maintain Dispute Resolution's Integrity?
<--- Score

103. How are you doing compared to your industry?
<--- Score

104. Will there be any necessary staff changes (redundancies or new hires)?
<--- Score

105. How will you insure seamless interoperability of Dispute Resolution moving forward?
<--- Score

106. How will you ensure you get what you expected?

<--- Score

107. Who else should you help?
<--- Score

108. If you had to leave your organization for a year and the only communication you could have with employees/colleagues was a single paragraph, what would you write?
<--- Score

109. What Dispute Resolution modifications can you make work for you?
<--- Score

110. What new services of functionality will be implemented next with Dispute Resolution ?
<--- Score

111. Political -is anyone trying to undermine this project?
<--- Score

112. Who is responsible for ensuring appropriate resources (time, people and money) are allocated to Dispute Resolution?
<--- Score

113. What stupid rule would you most like to kill?
<--- Score

114. Are all key stakeholders present at all Structured Walkthroughs?
<--- Score

115. How do you assess the Dispute Resolution pitfalls

that are inherent in implementing it?
<--- Score

116. Can you break it down?
<--- Score

117. Do you have the right people on the bus?
<--- Score

118. What are internal and external Dispute Resolution relations?
<--- Score

119. What did you miss in the interview for the worst hire you ever made?
<--- Score

120. What is your formula for success in Dispute Resolution ?
<--- Score

121. What happens if you do not have enough funding?
<--- Score

122. What unique value proposition (UVP) do you offer?
<--- Score

123. Are your responses positive or negative?
<--- Score

124. Who will determine interim and final deadlines?
<--- Score

125. To whom do you add value?

<--- Score

126. Whose voice (department, ethnic group, women, older workers, etc) might you have missed hearing from in your company, and how might you amplify this voice to create positive momentum for your business?
<--- Score

127. What is the funding source for this project?
<--- Score

128. What relationships among Dispute Resolution trends do you perceive?
<--- Score

129. What are the challenges?
<--- Score

130. How do you engage the workforce, in addition to satisfying them?
<--- Score

131. What are the gaps in your knowledge and experience?
<--- Score

132. Who is responsible for Dispute Resolution?
<--- Score

133. Who do you think the world wants your organization to be?
<--- Score

134. In retrospect, of the projects that you pulled the plug on, what percent do you wish had been allowed

to keep going, and what percent do you wish had ended earlier?
<--- Score

135. How do you transition from the baseline to the target?
<--- Score

136. Do you know what you are doing? And who do you call if you don't?
<--- Score

137. What is the estimated value of the project?
<--- Score

138. Can you do all this work?
<--- Score

139. Have new benefits been realized?
<--- Score

140. Why is Dispute Resolution important for you now?
<--- Score

141. How do you go about securing Dispute Resolution?
<--- Score

142. What is the kind of project structure that would be appropriate for your Dispute Resolution project, should it be formal and complex, or can it be less formal and relatively simple?
<--- Score

143. What threat is Dispute Resolution addressing?

<--- Score

144. Are you satisfied with your current role? If not, what is missing from it?
<--- Score

145. Who will provide the final approval of Dispute Resolution deliverables?
<--- Score

146. How do you keep records, of what?
<--- Score

147. Do you have an implicit bias for capital investments over people investments?
<--- Score

148. If you got fired and a new hire took your place, what would she do different?
<--- Score

149. How do you set Dispute Resolution stretch targets and how do you get people to not only participate in setting these stretch targets but also that they strive to achieve these?
<--- Score

150. What was the last experiment you ran?
<--- Score

151. Would you rather sell to knowledgeable and informed customers or to uninformed customers?
<--- Score

152. How important is Dispute Resolution to the user organizations mission?

<--- Score

153. If no one would ever find out about your accomplishments, how would you lead differently?
<--- Score

154. Have benefits been optimized with all key stakeholders?
<--- Score

155. What role does communication play in the success or failure of a Dispute Resolution project?
<--- Score

156. How do you track customer value, profitability or financial return, organizational success, and sustainability?
<--- Score

157. What is the overall talent health of your organization as a whole at senior levels, and for each organization reporting to a member of the Senior Leadership Team?
<--- Score

158. What is the recommended frequency of auditing?
<--- Score

159. Do you see more potential in people than they do in themselves?
<--- Score

160. What are the key enablers to make this Dispute Resolution move?
<--- Score

161. Who is on the team?
<--- Score

162. Has implementation been effective in reaching specified objectives so far?
<--- Score

163. Ask yourself: how would you do this work if you only had one staff member to do it?
<--- Score

164. If you had to rebuild your organization without any traditional competitive advantages (i.e., no killer technology, promising research, innovative product/ service delivery model, etcetera), how would your people have to approach their work and collaborate together in order to create the necessary conditions for success?
<--- Score

165. How do you stay inspired?
<--- Score

166. What Dispute Resolution skills are most important?
<--- Score

167. Are you relevant? Will you be relevant five years from now? Ten?
<--- Score

168. What are the rules and assumptions your industry operates under? What if the opposite were true?
<--- Score

169. Can you maintain your growth without

detracting from the factors that have contributed to your success?
<--- Score

170. What are you challenging?
<--- Score

171. Instead of going to current contacts for new ideas, what if you reconnected with dormant contacts--the people you used to know? If you were going reactivate a dormant tie, who would it be?
<--- Score

172. What knowledge, skills and characteristics mark a good Dispute Resolution project manager?
<--- Score

173. How do you keep the momentum going?
<--- Score

174. What is your Dispute Resolution strategy?
<--- Score

175. Is your basic point _____ or _____?
<--- Score

176. What are the success criteria that will indicate that Dispute Resolution objectives have been met and the benefits delivered?
<--- Score

177. What trophy do you want on your mantle?
<--- Score

178. If you were responsible for initiating and implementing major changes in your organization,

what steps might you take to ensure acceptance of those changes?
<--- Score

179. Which individuals, teams or departments will be involved in Dispute Resolution?
<--- Score

180. Is it economical; do you have the time and money?
<--- Score

181. Are assumptions made in Dispute Resolution stated explicitly?
<--- Score

182. When information truly is ubiquitous, when reach and connectivity are completely global, when computing resources are infinite, and when a whole new set of impossibilities are not only possible, but happening, what will that do to your business?
<--- Score

183. How do you make it meaningful in connecting Dispute Resolution with what users do day-to-day?
<--- Score

184. How do you lead with Dispute Resolution in mind?
<--- Score

185. How do you know if you are successful?
<--- Score

186. What are the potential basics of Dispute Resolution fraud?

<--- Score

187. How can you become the company that would put you out of business?
<--- Score

188. Will it be accepted by users?
<--- Score

189. How is implementation research currently incorporated into each of your goals?
<--- Score

190. Who will manage the integration of tools?
<--- Score

191. How do you accomplish your long range Dispute Resolution goals?
<--- Score

192. What potential megatrends could make your business model obsolete?
<--- Score

193. What is it like to work for you?
<--- Score

194. What is the big Dispute Resolution idea?
<--- Score

195. Are you / should you be revolutionary or evolutionary?
<--- Score

196. What information is critical to your organization that your executives are ignoring?

<--- Score

197. Is Dispute Resolution realistic, or are you setting yourself up for failure?
<--- Score

198. In the past year, what have you done (or could you have done) to increase the accurate perception of your company/brand as ethical and honest?
<--- Score

199. What do we do when new problems arise?
<--- Score

200. Is there a work around that you can use?
<--- Score

201. Do you think you know, or do you know you know ?
<--- Score

202. Is there any reason to believe the opposite of my current belief?
<--- Score

203. How does Dispute Resolution integrate with other stakeholder initiatives?
<--- Score

204. Why do and why don't your customers like your organization?
<--- Score

205. What management system can you use to leverage the Dispute Resolution experience, ideas, and concerns of the people closest to the work to be

done?
<--- Score

206. If you do not follow, then how to lead?
<--- Score

207. Are you paying enough attention to the partners your company depends on to succeed?
<--- Score

208. What should you stop doing?
<--- Score

209. Do you have the right capabilities and capacities?
<--- Score

210. If you find that you havent accomplished one of the goals for one of the steps of the Dispute Resolution strategy, what will you do to fix it?
<--- Score

211. Who is responsible for errors?
<--- Score

212. What is your competitive advantage?
<--- Score

213. Can the schedule be done in the given time?
<--- Score

214. How do you provide a safe environment -physically and emotionally?
<--- Score

215. What is the range of capabilities?
<--- Score

216. What is your BATNA (best alternative to a negotiated agreement)?
<--- Score

217. Whom among your colleagues do you trust, and for what?
<--- Score

218. Are the assumptions believable and achievable?
<--- Score

219. What is the source of the strategies for Dispute Resolution strengthening and reform?
<--- Score

220. What is an unauthorized commitment?
<--- Score

221. Why should people listen to you?
<--- Score

222. Do you have enough freaky customers in your portfolio pushing you to the limit day in and day out?
<--- Score

223. At what moment would you think; Will I get fired?
<--- Score

224. Why should you adopt a Dispute Resolution framework?
<--- Score

225. What are the barriers to increased Dispute Resolution production?
<--- Score

226. What is the purpose of Dispute Resolution in relation to the mission?
<--- Score

227. Who uses your product in ways you never expected?
<--- Score

228. What are your most important goals for the strategic Dispute Resolution objectives?
<--- Score

229. Who are your customers?
<--- Score

230. Is a Dispute Resolution breakthrough on the horizon?
<--- Score

231. If there were zero limitations, what would you do differently?
<--- Score

232. Is a Dispute Resolution team work effort in place?
<--- Score

233. How do you govern and fulfill your societal responsibilities?
<--- Score

Add up total points for this section:
_____ = Total points for this section

Divided by: _____ (number of statements answered) = _____

Average score for this section

Transfer your score to the Dispute
Resolution Index at the beginning of
the Self-Assessment.

Dispute Resolution and Managing Projects, Criteria for Project Managers:

1.0 Initiating Process Group: Dispute Resolution

1. What were things that you did very well and want to do the same again on the next Dispute Resolution project?

2. What will you do to minimize the impact should a risk event occur?

3. If action is called for, what form should it take?

4. What areas were overlooked on this Dispute Resolution project?

5. When are the deliverables to be generated in each phase?

6. Do you know the roles & responsibilities required for this Dispute Resolution project?

7. The Dispute Resolution project you are managing has nine stakeholders. How many channel of communications are there between corresponding stakeholders?

8. Were escalated issues resolved promptly?

9. Were sponsors and decision makers available when needed outside regularly scheduled meetings?

10. At which stage, in a typical Dispute Resolution project do stake holders have maximum influence?

11. The Dispute Resolution project managers have

maximum authority in which type of organization?

12. Did you use a contractor or vendor?

13. Establishment of pm office?

14. Are stakeholders properly informed about the status of the Dispute Resolution project?

15. Information sharing?

16. Are identified risks being monitored properly, are new risks arising during the Dispute Resolution project or are foreseen risks occurring?

17. Contingency planning. if a risk event occurs, what will you do?

18. What is the NEXT thing to do?

19. How well did the chosen processes fit the needs of the Dispute Resolution project?

20. The process to Manage Stakeholders is part of which process group?

1.1 Project Charter: Dispute Resolution

21. Who manages integration?

22. Why Outsource?

23. When do you use a Dispute Resolution project Charter?

24. How are Dispute Resolution projects different from operations?

25. Why executive support?

26. Dispute Resolution project background: what is the primary motivation for this Dispute Resolution project?

27. Will this replace an existing product?

28. What is in it for you?

29. Dependent Dispute Resolution projects: what Dispute Resolution projects must be underway or completed before this Dispute Resolution project can be successful?

30. How much?

31. For whom?

32. What metrics could you look at?

33. What are the assumptions?

34. Does the Dispute Resolution project need to consider any special capacity or capability issues?

35. What is the business need?

36. What are some examples of a business case?

37. Why have you chosen the aim you have set forth?

38. What outcome, in measureable terms, are you hoping to accomplish?

39. Why the improvements?

40. Who will take notes, document decisions?

1.2 Stakeholder Register: Dispute Resolution

41. What is the power of the stakeholder?

42. How big is the gap?

43. How should employers make voices heard?

44. Is your organization ready for change?

45. Who wants to talk about Security?

46. What & Why?

47. Who are the stakeholders?

48. Who is managing stakeholder engagement?

49. What opportunities exist to provide communications?

50. How will reports be created?

51. How much influence do they have on the Dispute Resolution project?

52. What are the major Dispute Resolution project milestones requiring communications or providing communications opportunities?

1.3 Stakeholder Analysis Matrix: Dispute Resolution

53. Do the stakeholders goals and expectations support or conflict with the Dispute Resolution project goals?

54. Who determines value?

55. Sustaining internal capabilities?

56. Timescales, deadlines and pressures?

57. What actions can be taken to reduce or mitigate risk?

58. How much do resources cost?

59. What is social & public accountability ?

60. What is the stakeholders power and status in relation to the Dispute Resolution project?

61. Price, value, quality?

62. How will the Dispute Resolution project benefit them?

63. Experience, knowledge, data?

64. Identify the stakeholders levels most frequently used –or at least sought– in your Dispute Resolution projects and for which purpose?

65. What is your Advocacy Strategy?

66. Who is influential in the Dispute Resolution project area (both thematic and geographic areas)?

67. Who is most interested in information about the topic and/or has previously initiated interest?

68. Who is most dependent on the resources at stake?

69. Why is it important to identify them?

70. Who will promote/support the Dispute Resolution project, provided that they are involved?

71. What tools would help you communicate?

2.0 Planning Process Group: Dispute Resolution

72. How will you do it?

73. How are it Dispute Resolution projects different?

74. What is a Software Development Life Cycle (SDLC)?

75. Are there efficient coordination mechanisms to avoid overloading the counterparts, participating stakeholders?

76. Does the program have follow-up mechanisms (to verify the quality of the products, punctuality of delivery, etc.) to measure progress in the achievement of the envisaged results?

77. How many days can task X be late in starting without affecting the Dispute Resolution project completion date?

78. Product breakdown structure (pbs): what is the Dispute Resolution project result or product, and how should it look like, what are its parts?

79. How will users learn how to use the deliverables?

80. Professionals want to know what is expected from them; what are the deliverables?

81. What is the difference between the early schedule and late schedule?

82. In which Dispute Resolution project management process group is the detailed Dispute Resolution project budget created?

83. What factors are contributing to progress or delay in the achievement of products and results?

84. In what way has the program contributed towards the issue culture and development included on the public agenda?

85. To what extent is the program helping to influence your organizations policy framework?

86. In what ways can the governance of the Dispute Resolution project be improved so that it has greater likelihood of achieving future sustainability?

87. Why do it Dispute Resolution projects fail?

88. Are the follow-up indicators relevant and do they meet the quality needed to measure the outputs and outcomes of the Dispute Resolution project?

89. Does it make any difference if you are successful?

90. Did the program design/ implementation strategy adequately address the planning stage necessary to set up structures, hire staff etc.?

2.1 Project Management Plan: Dispute Resolution

91. Are the existing and future without-plan conditions reasonable and appropriate?

92. Who is the Dispute Resolution project Manager?

93. What worked well?

94. How do you organize the costs in the Dispute Resolution project management plan?

95. How can you best help your organization to develop consistent practices in Dispute Resolution project management planning stages?

96. What data/reports/tools/etc. do program managers need?

97. Are calculations and results of analyzes essentially correct?

98. Does the implementation plan have an appropriate division of responsibilities?

99. What did not work so well?

100. Do the proposed changes from the Dispute Resolution project include any significant risks to safety?

101. Are there any windfall benefits that would accrue

to the Dispute Resolution project sponsor or other parties?

102. How do you manage integration?

103. What happened during the process that you found interesting?

104. How well are you able to manage your risk?

105. Is mitigation authorized or recommended?

106. What are the known stakeholder requirements?

107. Is the budget realistic?

108. Where does all this information come from?

2.2 Scope Management Plan: Dispute Resolution

109. Is there an approved case?

110. What problem is being solved by delivering this Dispute Resolution project?

111. Who is doing what for whom?

112. Are the quality tools and methods identified in the Quality Plan appropriate to the Dispute Resolution project?

113. Is an industry recognized mechanized support tool(s) being used for Dispute Resolution project scheduling & tracking?

114. Are metrics used to evaluate and manage Vendors?

115. Does the Dispute Resolution project have a Quality Culture?

116. Are Dispute Resolution project contact logs kept up to date?

117. Has the Dispute Resolution project manager been identified?

118. Cost / benefit analysis?

119. What happens to rejected deliverables?

120. Is there an issues management plan in place?

121. Pop quiz – which are the same inputs as in scope planning?

122. Has the scope management document been updated and distributed to help prevent scope creep?

123. Does all Dispute Resolution project documentation reside in a common repository for easy access?

124. Do you keep stake holders informed?

125. Are the appropriate IT resources adequate to meet planned commitments?

126. Are all key components of a Quality Assurance Plan present?

127. Does the quality assurance process provide objective verification of adherence to applicable standards, procedures & requirements?

2.3 Requirements Management Plan: Dispute Resolution

128. Are all the stakeholders ready for the transition into the user community?

129. Did you avoid subjective, flowery or non-specific statements?

130. What is a problem?

131. Is the system software (non-operating system) new to the IT Dispute Resolution project team?

132. Who is responsible for monitoring and tracking the Dispute Resolution project requirements?

133. Is there formal agreement on who has authority to request a change in requirements?

134. Is the system software (non-operating system) new to the IT Dispute Resolution project team?

135. What went wrong?

136. Do you expect stakeholders to be cooperative?

137. Is infrastructure setup part of your Dispute Resolution project?

138. When and how will a requirements baseline be established in this Dispute Resolution project?

139. Who has the authority to reject Dispute Resolution project requirements?

140. The wbs is developed as part of a joint planning session. and how do you know that youhave done this right?

141. What is the earliest finish date for this Dispute Resolution project if it is scheduled to start on ...?

142. Is stakeholder risk tolerance an important factor for the requirements process in this Dispute Resolution project?

143. How detailed should the Dispute Resolution project get?

144. Describe the process for rejecting the Dispute Resolution project requirements. Who has the authority to reject Dispute Resolution project requirements?

145. Does the Dispute Resolution project have a Change Control process?

146. How will the information be distributed?

147. Who will approve the requirements (and if multiple approvers, in what order)?

2.4 Requirements Documentation: Dispute Resolution

148. What is effective documentation?

149. How will requirements be documented and who signs off on them?

150. What can tools do for us?

151. Where are business rules being captured?

152. Who provides requirements?

153. Is the requirement properly understood?

154. Where do system and software requirements come from, what are sources?

155. How can you document system requirements?

156. What is your Elevator Speech?

157. Do your constraints stand?

158. Who is interacting with the system?

159. What is the risk associated with cost and schedule?

160. Consistency. are there any requirements conflicts?

161. Does the system provide the functions which best support the customers needs?

162. How does what is being described meet the business need?

163. What is the risk associated with the technology?

164. Can the requirement be changed without a large impact on other requirements?

165. Verifiability. can the requirements be checked?

166. Is the origin of the requirement clearly stated?

167. What are the potential disadvantages/ advantages?

2.5 Requirements Traceability Matrix: Dispute Resolution

168. What is the WBS?

169. Why use a WBS?

170. Is there a requirements traceability process in place?

171. How will it affect the stakeholders personally in career?

172. Do you have a clear understanding of all subcontracts in place?

173. How do you manage scope?

174. Describe the process for approving requirements so they can be added to the traceability matrix and Dispute Resolution project work can be performed. Will the Dispute Resolution project requirements become approved in writing?

175. How small is small enough?

176. What are the chronologies, contingencies, consequences, criteria?

177. What percentage of Dispute Resolution projects are producing traceability matrices between requirements and other work products?

178. Will you use a Requirements Traceability Matrix?

179. Why do you manage scope?

2.6 Project Scope Statement: Dispute Resolution

180. Have you been able to easily identify success criteria and create objective measurements for each of the Dispute Resolution project scopes goal statements?

181. Change management vs. change leadership - what is the difference?

182. Were potential customers involved early in the planning process?

183. Is the Dispute Resolution project organization documented and on file?

184. Are the input requirements from the team members clearly documented and communicated?

185. What are the defined meeting materials?

186. If there are vendors, have they signed off on the Dispute Resolution project Plan?

187. Elements that deal with providing the detail?

188. Have you been able to thoroughly document the Dispute Resolution projects assumptions and constraints?

189. If the scope changes, what will the impact be to your Dispute Resolution project in terms of duration,

cost, quality, or any other important areas of the Dispute Resolution project?

190. Will you need a statement of work?

191. What are the possible consequences should a risk come to occur?

192. Is there a Quality Assurance Plan documented and filed?

193. Will all Dispute Resolution project issues be unconditionally tracked through the issue resolution process?

194. Is the plan under configuration management?

195. Has everyone approved the Dispute Resolution projects scope statement?

196. Are there completion/verification criteria defined for each task producing an output?

197. Will this process be communicated to the customer and Dispute Resolution project team?

198. What went right?

199. Relevant - ask yourself can you get there; why are you doing this Dispute Resolution project?

2.7 Assumption and Constraint Log: Dispute Resolution

200. Are best practices and metrics employed to identify issues, progress, performance, etc.?

201. Are there ways to reduce the time it takes to get something approved?

202. Is staff trained on the software technologies that are being used on the Dispute Resolution project?

203. Diagrams and tables are included to account for complex concepts and increase overall readability?

204. Are you meeting your customers expectations consistently?

205. How relevant is this attribute to this Dispute Resolution project or audit?

206. How can you prevent/fix violations?

207. Are there cosmetic errors that hinder readability and comprehension?

208. No superfluous information or marketing narrative?

209. After observing execution of process, is it in compliance with the documented Plan?

210. What other teams / processes would be impacted

by changes to the current process, and how?

211. When can log be discarded?

212. What strengths do you have?

213. Does a specific action and/or state that is known to violate security policy occur?

214. What weaknesses do you have?

215. Contradictory information between different documents?

216. Is the definition of the Dispute Resolution project scope clear; what needs to be accomplished?

217. What do you audit?

218. Has a Dispute Resolution project Communications Plan been developed?

2.8 Work Breakdown Structure: Dispute Resolution

219. Is it a change in scope?

220. When do you stop?

221. Where does it take place?

222. When would you develop a Work Breakdown Structure?

223. Do you need another level?

224. Why would you develop a Work Breakdown Structure?

225. How much detail?

226. How far down?

227. What is the probability that the Dispute Resolution project duration will exceed xx weeks?

228. Can you make it?

229. How big is a work-package?

230. How will you and your Dispute Resolution project team define the Dispute Resolution projects scope and work breakdown structure?

231. What is the probability of completing the Dispute

Resolution project in less that xx days?

232. What has to be done?

233. Why is it useful?

234. When does it have to be done?

235. How many levels?

236. Who has to do it?

2.9 WBS Dictionary: Dispute Resolution

237. Are work packages reasonably short in time duration or do they have adequate objective indicators/milestones to minimize subjectivity of the in process work evaluation?

238. Cwbs elements to be subcontracted, with identification of subcontractors?

239. Does the contractor have procedures which permit identification of recurring or non-recurring costs as necessary?

240. Are all elements of indirect expense identified to overhead cost budgets of Dispute Resolution projections?

241. What is the goal?

242. How detailed should a Dispute Resolution project get?

243. Are time-phased budgets established for planning and control of level of effort activity by category of resource; for example, type of manpower and/or material?

244. Does the contractors system provide for accurate cost accumulation and assignment to control accounts in a manner consistent with the budgets using recognized acceptable costing techniques?

245. What are you counting on?

246. Does the contractor use objective results, design reviews and tests to trace schedule performance?

247. Are direct or indirect cost adjustments being accomplished according to accounting procedures acceptable to us?

248. Are the wbs and organizational levels for application of the Dispute Resolution projected overhead costs identified?

249. Are data elements (BCWS, BCWP, and ACWP) progressively summarized from the detail level to the contract level through the CWBS?

250. Are estimates of costs at completion utilized in determining contract funding requirements and reporting them?

251. Does the contractors system provide for determination of price variance by comparing planned Vs actual commitments?

252. Is all budget available as management reserve identified and excluded from the performance measurement baseline?

253. Are management actions taken to reduce indirect costs when there are significant adverse variances?

254. Does the scheduling system provide for the identification of work progress against technical and

other milestones, and also provide for forecasts of completion dates of scheduled work?

255. Do the lines of authority for incurring indirect costs correspond to the lines of responsibility for management control of the same components of costs?

256. Changes in the overhead pool and/or organization structures?

2.10 Schedule Management Plan: Dispute Resolution

257. Are the processes for schedule assessment and analysis defined?

258. Is there any form of automated support for Issues Management?

259. Are there checklists created to determine if all quality processes are followed?

260. Are mitigation strategies identified?

261. Are trade-offs between accepting the risk and mitigating the risk identified?

262. Does the ims reflect accurate current status and credible start/finish forecasts for all to-go tasks and milestones?

263. Are updated Dispute Resolution project time & resource estimates reasonable based on the current Dispute Resolution project stage?

264. Have all involved Dispute Resolution project stakeholders and work groups committed to the Dispute Resolution project?

265. Is the schedule vertically and horizontally traceable?

266. Has the ims content been baselined and is it

adequately controlled?

267. Does the detailed work plan match the complexity of tasks with the capabilities of personnel?

268. Are non-critical path items updated and agreed upon with the teams?

269. Is the quality assurance team identified?

270. Is a pmo (Dispute Resolution project management office) in place and provide oversight to the Dispute Resolution project?

271. Are multiple estimation methods being employed?

272. Are the predecessor and successor relationships accurate?

273. Are all activities captured and do they address all approved work scope in the Dispute Resolution project baseline?

274. Is it standard practice to formally commit stakeholders to the Dispute Resolution project via agreements?

2.11 Activity List: Dispute Resolution

275. How can the Dispute Resolution project be displayed graphically to better visualize the activities?

276. How detailed should a Dispute Resolution project get?

277. What is the probability the Dispute Resolution project can be completed in xx weeks?

278. Should you include sub-activities?

279. What did not go as well?

280. How difficult will it be to do specific activities on this Dispute Resolution project?

281. When do the individual activities need to start and finish?

282. In what sequence?

283. When will the work be performed?

284. Is infrastructure setup part of your Dispute Resolution project?

285. What will be performed?

286. Can you determine the activity that must finish, before this activity can start?

287. How should ongoing costs be monitored to try to

keep the Dispute Resolution project within budget?

288. What is your organizations history in doing similar activities?

289. Are the required resources available or need to be acquired?

290. What are the critical bottleneck activities?

291. Is there anything planned that does not need to be here?

292. How will it be performed?

2.12 Activity Attributes: Dispute Resolution

293. How else could the items be grouped?

294. Activity: fair or not fair?

295. Would you consider either of corresponding activities an outlier?

296. Does your organization of the data change its meaning?

297. How many resources do you need to complete the work scope within a limit of X number of days?

298. How many days do you need to complete the work scope with a limit of X number of resources?

299. How do you manage time?

300. Can more resources be added?

301. What is the general pattern here?

302. How difficult will it be to do specific activities on this Dispute Resolution project?

303. Activity: what is Missing?

304. Resources to accomplish the work?

305. Were there other ways you could have organized

the data to achieve similar results?

306. Resource is assigned to?

307. How difficult will it be to complete specific activities on this Dispute Resolution project?

308. Have constraints been applied to the start and finish milestones for the phases?

309. Time for overtime?

310. What is missing?

2.13 Milestone List: Dispute Resolution

311. Environmental effects?

312. Gaps in capabilities?

313. Can you derive how soon can the whole Dispute Resolution project finish?

314. How will the milestone be verified?

315. Who will manage the Dispute Resolution project on a day-to-day basis?

316. Reliability of data, plan predictability?

317. Calculate how long can activity be delayed?

318. Continuity, supply chain robustness?

319. When will the Dispute Resolution project be complete?

320. Vital contracts and partners?

321. Insurmountable weaknesses?

322. Obstacles faced?

323. Global influences?

324. What specific improvements did you make to

the Dispute Resolution project proposal since the previous time?

325. Identify critical paths (one or more) and which activities are on the critical path?

326. What background experience, skills, and strengths does the team bring to your organization?

327. How soon can the activity start?

2.14 Network Diagram: Dispute Resolution

328. What activity must be completed immediately before this activity can start?

329. What is the completion time?

330. Can you calculate the confidence level?

331. Where do you schedule uncertainty time?

332. What to do and When?

333. Are you on time?

334. Which type of network diagram allows you to depict four types of dependencies?

335. What activities must occur simultaneously with this activity?

336. Why must you schedule milestones, such as reviews, throughout the Dispute Resolution project?

337. What is the lowest cost to complete this Dispute Resolution project in xx weeks?

338. Where do schedules come from?

339. What can be done concurrently?

340. Exercise: what is the probability that the Dispute

Resolution project duration will exceed xx weeks?

341. What job or jobs precede it?

342. What is the probability of completing the Dispute Resolution project in less that xx days?

343. How confident can you be in your milestone dates and the delivery date?

344. What controls the start and finish of a job?

345. What are the Major Administrative Issues?

346. What activities must follow this activity?

2.15 Activity Resource Requirements: Dispute Resolution

347. What is the Work Plan Standard?

348. How do you handle petty cash?

349. Which logical relationship does the PDM use most often?

350. Why do you do that?

351. Are there unresolved issues that need to be addressed?

352. When does monitoring begin?

353. How many signatures do you require on a check and does this match what is in your policy and procedures?

354. What are constraints that you might find during the Human Resource Planning process?

355. Anything else?

356. Do you use tools like decomposition and rolling-wave planning to produce the activity list and other outputs?

357. Organizational Applicability?

358. Other support in specific areas?

2.16 Resource Breakdown Structure: Dispute Resolution

359. What is the difference between % Complete and % work?

360. Why time management?

361. Who delivers the information?

362. Which resource planning tool provides information on resource responsibility and accountability?

363. Who will be used as a Dispute Resolution project team member?

364. What is each stakeholders desired outcome for the Dispute Resolution project?

365. The list could probably go on, but, the thing that you would most like to know is, How long & How much?

366. What is Dispute Resolution project communication management?

367. How can this help you with team building?

368. What is the primary purpose of the human resource plan?

369. Who needs what information?

370. Who is allowed to see what data about which resources?

371. Any changes from stakeholders?

372. Are the required resources available?

373. Is predictive resource analysis being done?

374. What can you do to improve productivity?

375. Which resources should be in the resource pool?

2.17 Activity Duration Estimates: Dispute Resolution

376. Will outside resources be needed to help in its development?

377. What tasks can take place concurrently?

378. Does the case present a realistic scenario?

379. Are Dispute Resolution project results verified and Dispute Resolution project documents archived?

380. How does the job market and current state of the economy affect human resource management?

381. Are procedures defined for calculating cost estimates?

382. What are the three main outputs of quality control?

383. Are procurement documents used to solicit accurate and complete proposals from prospective sellers?

384. Write a oneto two-page paper describing your dream team for this Dispute Resolution project. What type of people would you want on your team?

385. How can you use Microsoft Dispute Resolution project and Excel to assist in Dispute Resolution project risk management?

386. Dispute Resolution project manager has received activity duration estimates from his team. Which does one need in order to complete schedule development?

387. How could you define throughput and how would your organization benefit from maximizing it?

388. Is training acquired to enhance the skills, knowledge and capabilities of the Dispute Resolution project team?

389. What should be done NEXT?

390. Are Dispute Resolution project activities decomposed into manageable components to ensure expected management control?

391. What type of contract was used and why?

392. Are time, scope, cost, and quality monitored throughout the Dispute Resolution project?

393. What Dispute Resolution project was the first to use modern Dispute Resolution project management?

394. Are changes to the scope managed according to defined procedures?

395. What functions does this software provide that cannot be done easily using other tools such as a spreadsheet or database?

2.18 Duration Estimating Worksheet: Dispute Resolution

396. Value pocket identification & quantification what are value pockets?

397. How can the Dispute Resolution project be displayed graphically to better visualize the activities?

398. Why estimate costs?

399. When, then?

400. What is cost and Dispute Resolution project cost management?

401. Why estimate time and cost?

402. What is an Average Dispute Resolution project?

403. What is the total time required to complete the Dispute Resolution project if no delays occur?

404. Will the Dispute Resolution project collaborate with the local community and leverage resources?

405. What questions do you have?

406. What is your role?

407. Done before proceeding with this activity or what can be done concurrently?

408. Does the Dispute Resolution project provide innovative ways for stakeholders to overcome obstacles or deliver better outcomes?

409. For other activities, how much delay can be tolerated?

410. What is next?

411. What work will be included in the Dispute Resolution project?

412. Can the Dispute Resolution project be constructed as planned?

2.19 Project Schedule: Dispute Resolution

413. Your best shot for providing estimations how complex/how much work does the activity require?

414. Was the Dispute Resolution project schedule reviewed by all stakeholders and formally accepted?

415. What is the difference?

416. Did the final product meet or exceed user expectations?

417. How can you address that situation?

418. Should you have a test for each code module?

419. How do you know that youhave done this right?

420. What is risk?

421. Are all remaining durations correct?

422. Did the Dispute Resolution project come in on schedule?

423. Why or why not?

424. How can slack be negative?

425. Does the condition or event threaten the Dispute Resolution projects objectives in any ways?

426. Verify that the update is accurate. Are all remaining durations correct?

427. Is the structure for tracking the Dispute Resolution project schedule well defined and assigned to a specific individual?

428. Month Dispute Resolution project take?

2.20 Cost Management Plan: Dispute Resolution

429. Milestones – what are the key dates in executing the contract plan?

430. Contractors scope – how will contractors scope be defined when contracts are let?

431. Have all documents been archived in a Dispute Resolution project repository for each release?

432. What threats might prevent you from getting there?

433. Are any non-compliance issues that exist due to State practices communicated to your organization?

434. Does the Dispute Resolution project have a formal Dispute Resolution project Charter?

435. Schedule variances – how will schedule variances be identified and corrected?

436. Weve met your goals?

437. Are Dispute Resolution project leaders committed to this Dispute Resolution project full time?

438. Is it possible to track all classes of Dispute Resolution project work (e.g. scheduled, un-scheduled, defect repair, etc.)?

439. Is your organization certified as a supplier, wholesaler and/or regular dealer?

440. Are the people assigned to the Dispute Resolution project sufficiently qualified?

441. Forecasts – how will the cost to complete the Dispute Resolution project be forecast?

442. Do all stakeholders know how to access this repository and where to find the Dispute Resolution project documentation?

443. For cost control purposes?

444. Are all payments made according to the contract(s)?

445. Is a stakeholder management plan in place that covers topics?

446. Has the business need been clearly defined?

2.21 Activity Cost Estimates: Dispute Resolution

447. How do you manage cost?

448. What areas were overlooked on this Dispute Resolution project?

449. What is the last item a Dispute Resolution project manager must do to finalize Dispute Resolution project close-out?

450. Were you satisfied with the work?

451. How do you treat administrative costs in the activity inventory?

452. How do you change activities?

453. Who & what determines the need for contracted services?

454. What is the Dispute Resolution projects sustainability strategy that will ensure Dispute Resolution project results will endure or be sustained?

455. What is included in indirect cost being allocated?

456. What is your organizations history in doing similar tasks?

457. What is the activity inventory?

458. Will you need to provide essential services information about activities?

459. How do you fund change orders?

460. Maintenance Reserve?

461. Who determines when the contractor is paid?

462. If you are asked to lower your estimate because the price is too high, what are your options?

463. What were things that you need to improve?

464. Did the consultant work with local staff to develop local capacity?

465. How do you allocate indirect costs to activities?

466. Would you hire them again?

2.22 Cost Estimating Worksheet: Dispute Resolution

467. Can a trend be established from historical performance data on the selected measure and are the criteria for using trend analysis or forecasting methods met?

468. What costs are to be estimated?

469. What is the estimated labor cost today based upon this information?

470. Is the Dispute Resolution project responsive to community need?

471. Identify the timeframe necessary to monitor progress and collect data to determine how the selected measure has changed?

472. What happens to any remaining funds not used?

473. Does the Dispute Resolution project provide innovative ways for stakeholders to overcome obstacles or deliver better outcomes?

474. What can be included?

475. Who is best positioned to know and assist in identifying corresponding factors?

476. What is the purpose of estimating?

477. Will the Dispute Resolution project collaborate with the local community and leverage resources?

478. What info is needed?

479. What will others want?

480. How will the results be shared and to whom?

481. Ask: are others positioned to know, are others credible, and will others cooperate?

482. Is it feasible to establish a control group arrangement?

483. What additional Dispute Resolution project(s) could be initiated as a result of this Dispute Resolution project?

2.23 Cost Baseline: Dispute Resolution

484. Is there anything you need from upper management in order to be successful?

485. Dispute Resolution project goals -should others be reconsidered?

486. Pcs for your new business. what would the life cycle costs be?

487. Has the Dispute Resolution project (or Dispute Resolution project phase) been evaluated against each objective established in the product description and Integrated Dispute Resolution project Plan?

488. Are procedures defined by which the cost baseline may be changed?

489. Has the actual cost of the Dispute Resolution project (or Dispute Resolution project phase) been tallied and compared to the approved budget?

490. What can go wrong?

491. Why do you manage cost?

492. Has the appropriate access to relevant data and analysis capability been granted?

493. Is the requested change request a result of changes in other Dispute Resolution project(s)?

494. Verify business objectives. Are others appropriate, and well-articulated?

495. For what purpose ?

496. Has operations management formally accepted responsibility for operating and maintaining the product(s) or service(s) delivered by the Dispute Resolution project?

497. Where do changes come from?

498. Eac -estimate at completion, what is the total job expected to cost?

499. What deliverables come first?

500. Does a process exist for establishing a cost baseline to measure Dispute Resolution project performance?

501. Should a more thorough impact analysis be conducted?

502. What would the life cycle costs be?

2.24 Quality Management Plan: Dispute Resolution

503. How does your organization recruit, hire, and retain new employees?

504. Diagrams and tables to account for complex concepts and increase overall readability?

505. How is staff trained in procedures?

506. How is staff informed of proper reporting methods?

507. Why quality management?

508. How does your organization determine the requirements and product/service features important to customers?

509. What does it do for you (or to me)?

510. Does a prospective decision remain the same regardless of what the data show is?

511. Is staff trained on the software technologies that are being used on the Dispute Resolution project?

512. Were there any deficiencies / issues identified in the prior years self-assessment?

513. What process do you use to minimize errors, defects, and rework?

514. What is positive about the current process?

515. What are your key performance measures/ indicators for tracking progress relative to your action plans?

516. Does the program conduct field testing?

517. Who is responsible?

518. What data do you gather/use/compile?

519. Are you following the quality standards?

520. Are there trends or hot spots?

521. Were there any deficiencies / issues in prior years self-assessment?

522. Documented results available?

2.25 Quality Metrics: Dispute Resolution

523. If the defect rate during testing is substantially higher than that of the previous release (or a similar product), then ask: Did you plan for and actually improve testing effectiveness?

524. How do you measure?

525. Where is quality now?

526. What makes a visualization memorable?

527. What method of measurement do you use?

528. What are your organizations next steps?

529. Are there any open risk issues?

530. What is the CMS Benchmark?

531. Did the team meet the Dispute Resolution project success criteria documented in the Quality Metrics Matrix?

532. Is there a set of procedures to capture, analyze and act on quality metrics?

533. How do you communicate results and findings to upper management?

534. What is the benchmark?

535. What percentage are outcome-based?

536. Is there alignment within your organization on definitions?

537. How can the effectiveness of each of the activities be measured?

538. How do you know if everyone is trying to improve the right things?

539. Are quality metrics defined?

540. How do you calculate corresponding metrics?

541. How are requirements conflicts resolved?

2.26 Process Improvement Plan: Dispute Resolution

542. Are you making progress on the improvement framework?

543. Why do you want to achieve the goal?

544. What lessons have you learned so far?

545. What is the test-cycle concept?

546. Where are you now?

547. Management commitment at all levels?

548. Are you meeting the quality standards?

549. Who should prepare the process improvement action plan?

550. What personnel are the sponsors for that initiative?

551. What personnel are the champions for the initiative?

552. Where do you focus?

553. To elicit goal statements, do you ask a question such as, What do you want to achieve?

554. Where do you want to be?

555. Does your process ensure quality?

556. Have storage and access mechanisms and procedures been determined?

557. Has the time line required to move measurement results from the points of collection to databases or users been established?

558. Are you making progress on the goals?

2.27 Responsibility Assignment Matrix: Dispute Resolution

559. Is work properly classified as measured effort, LOE, or apportioned effort and appropriately separated?

560. Are people afraid to let you know when others are under allocated?

561. Who is the Dispute Resolution project Manager?

562. Is data disseminated to the contractors management timely, accurate, and usable?

563. Does the contractors system include procedures for measuring the performance of critical subcontractors?

564. Evaluate the performance of operating organizations?

565. Who is going to do that work?

566. All cwbs elements specified for external reporting?

567. Undistributed budgets, if any?

568. Competencies and craftsmanship – what competencies are necessary and what level?

569. What materials and procurements needed?

570. Does the contractors system provide unit or lot costs when applicable?

571. What expertise is available in your department?

572. What travel needed?

573. Do work packages consist of discrete tasks which are adequately described?

574. Are others working on the right things?

575. Will too many Communicating responsibilities tangle the Dispute Resolution project in unnecessary communications?

576. Are indirect costs charged to the appropriate indirect pools and incurring organization?

577. Are the overhead pools formally and adequately identified?

2.28 Roles and Responsibilities: Dispute Resolution

578. Attainable / achievable: the goal is attainable; can you actually accomplish the goal?

579. Where are you most strong as a supervisor?

580. What is working well within your organizations performance management system?

581. How well did the Dispute Resolution project Team understand the expectations of specific roles and responsibilities?

582. What expectations were met?

583. Accountabilities: what are the roles and responsibilities of individual team members?

584. What should you do now to prepare yourself for a promotion, increased responsibilities or a different job?

585. Are governance roles and responsibilities documented?

586. Once the responsibilities are defined for the Dispute Resolution project, have the deliverables, roles and responsibilities been clearly communicated to every participant?

587. Are your budgets supportive of a culture of

quality data?

588. Is feedback clearly communicated and non-judgmental?

589. Is there a training program in place for stakeholders covering expectations, roles and responsibilities and any addition knowledge others need to be good stakeholders?

590. What should you highlight for improvement?

591. Influence: what areas of organizational decision making are you able to influence when you do not have authority to make the final decision?

592. Is the data complete?

593. Required skills, knowledge, experience?

594. Be specific; avoid generalities. Thank you and great work alone are insufficient. What exactly do you appreciate and why?

595. Do you take the time to clearly define roles and responsibilities on Dispute Resolution project tasks?

596. Concern: where are you limited or have no authority, where you can not influence?

597. Who is responsible for each task?

2.29 Human Resource Management Plan: Dispute Resolution

598. Sensitivity analysis?

599. Were Dispute Resolution project team members involved in the development of activity & task decomposition?

600. What is the boss?

601. Does the business case include how the Dispute Resolution project aligns with your organizations strategic goals & objectives?

602. Is the steering committee active in Dispute Resolution project oversight?

603. Who will be impacted (both positively and negatively) as a result of or during the execution of this Dispute Resolution project?

604. Are corrective actions and variances reported?

605. Is the structure for tracking the Dispute Resolution project schedule well defined and assigned to a specific individual?

606. Was the scope definition used in task sequencing?

607. Are the quality tools and methods identified in the Quality Plan appropriate to the Dispute Resolution

project?

608. What did you have to assume to be true to complete the charter?

609. What were things that you did well, and could improve, and how?

610. How to convince employees that this is a necessary process?

611. Is a pmo (Dispute Resolution project management office) in place and provide oversight to the Dispute Resolution project?

612. Does the resource management plan include a personnel development plan?

613. Does all Dispute Resolution project documentation reside in a common repository for easy access?

614. Is there a formal set of procedures supporting Issues Management?

615. Are actuals compared against estimates to analyze and correct variances?

616. Is there a Steering Committee in place?

2.30 Communications Management Plan: Dispute Resolution

617. What data is going to be required?

618. Who is involved as you identify stakeholders?

619. Which stakeholders are thought leaders, influences, or early adopters?

620. Who did you turn to if you had questions?

621. Are there potential barriers between the team and the stakeholder?

622. Do you feel a register helps?

623. Who to learn from?

624. How were corresponding initiatives successful?

625. What to learn?

626. Will messages be directly related to the release strategy or phases of the Dispute Resolution project?

627. How will the person responsible for executing the communication item be notified?

628. What is the stakeholders level of authority?

629. What is the political influence?

630. Are you constantly rushing from meeting to meeting?

631. Are stakeholders internal or external?

632. Which stakeholders can influence others?

633. Are the stakeholders getting the information others need, are others consulted, are concerns addressed?

634. Why do you manage communications?

2.31 Risk Management Plan: Dispute Resolution

635. Workarounds are determined during which step of risk management?

636. Are certain activities taking a long time to complete?

637. Are formal technical reviews part of this process?

638. Is the process being followed?

639. Premium on reliability of product?

640. Have you worked with the customer in the past?

641. Are you working on the right risks?

642. Are the required plans included, such as nonstructural flood risk management plans?

643. How is implementation of risk actions performed?

644. Risk probability and impact: how will the probabilities and impacts of risk items be assessed?

645. Internal technical and management reviews?

646. Do you train all developers in the process?

647. Is the customer willing to establish rapid

communication links with the developer?

648. Can the Dispute Resolution project proceed without assuming the risk?

649. What things are likely to change?

650. Does the customer have a solid idea of what is required?

651. Are enough people available?

652. Can you stabilize dynamic risk factors?

653. What is the likelihood?

654. User involvement: do you have the right users?

2.32 Risk Register: Dispute Resolution

655. Manageability – have mitigations to the risk been identified?

656. Amongst the action plans and recommendations that you have to introduce are there some that could stop or delay the overall program?

657. Are there any knock-on effects/impact on any of the other areas?

658. What will be done?

659. What is the reason for current performance gaps and do the risks and opportunities identified previously account for this?

660. How well are risks controlled?

661. What evidence do you have to justify the likelihood score of the risk (audit, incident report, claim, complaints, inspection, internal review)?

662. What are you going to do to limit the Dispute Resolution projects risk exposure due to the identified risks?

663. Who is going to do it?

664. Is further information required before making a decision?

665. Severity Prediction?

666. When is it going to be done?

667. What is the appropriate level of risk management for this Dispute Resolution project?

668. What are your key risks/show istoppers and what is being done to manage them?

669. How could corresponding Risk affect the Dispute Resolution project in terms of cost and schedule?

670. What risks might negatively or positively affect achieving the Dispute Resolution project objectives?

671. Financial risk -can your organization afford to undertake the Dispute Resolution project?

672. What can be done about it?

673. Risk documentation: what reporting formats and processes will be used for risk management activities?

674. What are the major risks facing the Dispute Resolution project?

2.33 Probability and Impact Assessment: Dispute Resolution

675. Are trained personnel, including supervisors and Dispute Resolution project managers, available to handle such a large Dispute Resolution project?

676. What are the current requirements of the customer?

677. Do end-users have realistic expectations?

678. How carefully have the potential competitors been identified?

679. What are the current or emerging trends of culture?

680. What are the likely future requirements?

681. What should be the gestation period for the Dispute Resolution project with specific technology?

682. How do risks change during a Dispute Resolution project life cycle?

683. Are tools for analysis and design available?

684. Who are the international/overseas Dispute Resolution project partners (equipment supplier/supplier/consultant/contractor) for this Dispute Resolution project?

685. How is the risk management process used in practice?

686. Do the requirements require the creation of new algorithms?

687. Costs associated with late delivery or a defective product?

688. Who should be responsible for the monitoring and tracking of the indicators youhave identified?

689. Is it necessary to deeply assess all Dispute Resolution project risks?

690. Are the best people available?

691. Are end-users enthusiastically committed to the Dispute Resolution project and the system/product to be built?

692. Should the risk be taken at all?

2.34 Probability and Impact Matrix: Dispute Resolution

693. The customer requests a change to the Dispute Resolution project that would increase the Dispute Resolution project risk. Which should you do before ass the others?

694. Have you ascribed a level of confidence to every critical technical objective?

695. What would you do differently?

696. How are risks and risk management perceived in the Dispute Resolution project?

697. During Dispute Resolution project executing, a team member identifies a risk that is not in the risk register. What should you do?

698. Who is going to be the consortium leader?

699. What is the probability of the risk occurring?

700. Prioritized components/features?

701. What is the risk appetite?

702. Risk may be made during which step of risk management?

703. What is the likelihood of a breakthrough?

704. Maximize short-term return on investment?

705. Have top software and customer managers formally committed to support the Dispute Resolution project?

706. What would be the effect of slippage?

707. Do you have specific methods that you use for each phase of the process?

2.35 Risk Data Sheet: Dispute Resolution

708. What can you do?

709. Whom do you serve (customers)?

710. How reliable is the data source?

711. What do people affected think about the need for, and practicality of preventive measures?

712. What if client refuses?

713. What can happen?

714. What was measured?

715. What are you here for (Mission)?

716. What do you know?

717. What will be the consequences if the risk happens?

718. How can it happen?

719. What are you weak at and therefore need to do better?

720. Will revised controls lead to tolerable risk levels?

721. Has a sensitivity analysis been carried out?

722. Do effective diagnostic tests exist?

723. What were the Causes that contributed?

724. What is the environment within which you operate (social trends, economic, community values, broad based participation, national directions etc.)?

725. What will be the consequences if it happens?

726. Has the most cost-effective solution been chosen?

2.36 Procurement Management Plan: Dispute Resolution

727. Is the steering committee active in Dispute Resolution project oversight?

728. Are schedule deliverables actually delivered?

729. Based on your Dispute Resolution project communication management plan, what worked well?

730. Is the communication plan being followed?

731. What types of contracts will be used?

732. Are updated Dispute Resolution project time & resource estimates reasonable based on the current Dispute Resolution project stage?

733. Has a resource management plan been created?

734. Has the schedule been baselined?

735. Is it possible to track all classes of Dispute Resolution project work (e.g. scheduled, un-scheduled, defect repair, etc.)?

736. Is there a procurement management plan in place?

737. Are Dispute Resolution project leaders committed to this Dispute Resolution project full

time?

738. What are things that you need to improve?

739. Is Dispute Resolution project work proceeding in accordance with the original Dispute Resolution project schedule?

740. Are parking lot items captured?

741. Is the structure for tracking the Dispute Resolution project schedule well defined and assigned to a specific individual?

742. Similar Dispute Resolution projects?

2.37 Source Selection Criteria: Dispute Resolution

743. How do you encourage efficiency and consistency?

744. What risks were identified in the proposals?

745. Are considerations anticipated?

746. How do you consolidate reviews and analysis of evaluators?

747. What should a DRFP include?

748. What are the limitations on pre-competitive range communications?

749. Who is entitled to a debriefing?

750. How will you decide an evaluators write up is sufficient?

751. Is a letter of commitment from each proposed team member and key subcontractor included?

752. What are the most common types of rating systems?

753. How is past performance evaluated?

754. Have all evaluators been trained?

755. How do you ensure an integrated assessment of proposals?

756. What is the basis of an estimate and what assumptions were made?

757. When is it appropriate to issue a DRFP?

758. When is it appropriate to issue a Draft Request for Proposal (DRFP)?

759. Are responses to considerations adequate?

760. Can you reasonably estimate total organization requirements for the coming year?

761. What instructions should be provided regarding oral presentations?

762. How should oral presentations be prepared for?

2.38 Stakeholder Management Plan: Dispute Resolution

763. Have all unresolved risks been documented?

764. Are there any potential occupational health and safety issues due to the proposed purchases?

765. What is the general purpose in defining responsibilities of the already stated affiliated with the Dispute Resolution project?

766. Which risks pose the highest threat?

767. Are changes in scope (deliverable commitments) agreed to by all affected groups & individuals?

768. Is documentation created for communication with the suppliers and vendors?

769. Have Dispute Resolution project management standards and procedures been identified / established and documented?

770. Can the requirements be traced to the appropriate components of the solution, as well as test scripts?

771. Were the budget estimates reasonable?

772. Have all involved stakeholders and work groups committed to the Dispute Resolution project?

773. Are cause and effect determined for risks when they occur?

774. How many Dispute Resolution project staff does this specific process affect?

775. Has a structured approach been used to break work effort into manageable components (WBS)?

776. Has the Dispute Resolution project manager been identified?

777. Are there standards for code development?

778. Are written status reports provided on a designated frequent basis?

2.39 Change Management Plan: Dispute Resolution

779. What processes are in place to manage knowledge about the Dispute Resolution project?

780. What communication network would you use – informal or formal?

781. What is the negative impact of communicating too soon or too late?

782. Are there resource implications for your communications strategy?

783. What is the reason for the communication?

784. How can you best frame the message so that it addresses the audiences interests?

785. Would you need to tailor a special message for each segment of the audience?

786. What policies and procedures need to be changed?

787. What would be an estimate of the total cost for the activities required to carry out the change initiative?

788. Clearly articulate the overall business benefits of the Dispute Resolution project -why are you doing this now?

789. What are the specific target groups/audiences that will be impacted by this change?

790. Do the proposed users have access to the appropriate documentation?

791. What risks may occur upfront?

792. What new roles are needed?

793. What do you expect the target audience to do, say, think or feel as a result of this communication?

794. How much change management is needed?

795. What are the specific target groups / audience that will be impacted by this change?

796. Change invariability confront many relationships especially the already stated that require a set of behaviours What roles with in your organization are affected and how?

797. How far reaching in your organization is the change?

3.0 Executing Process Group: Dispute Resolution

798. What are the main parts of the scope statement?

799. Specific - is the objective clear in terms of what, how, when, and where the situation will be changed?

800. How can software assist in Dispute Resolution project communications?

801. What is the shortest possible time it will take to complete this Dispute Resolution project?

802. How well did the chosen processes fit the needs of the Dispute Resolution project?

803. What are the main processes included in Dispute Resolution project quality management?

804. What type of information goes in the quality assurance plan?

805. When is the appropriate time to bring the scorecard to Board meetings?

806. Why do you need a good WBS to use Dispute Resolution project management software?

807. What areas were overlooked on this Dispute Resolution project?

808. What is involved in the solicitation process?

809. What are the main types of contracts if you do decide to outsource?

810. When do you share the scorecard with managers?

811. Will new hardware or software be required for servers or client machines?

812. Have operating capacities been created and/or reinforced in partners?

813. Is the schedule for the set products being met?

814. How will you know you did it?

3.1 Team Member Status Report: Dispute Resolution

815. How much risk is involved?

816. Why is it to be done?

817. How does this product, good, or service meet the needs of the Dispute Resolution project and your organization as a whole?

818. What is to be done?

819. When a teams productivity and success depend on collaboration and the efficient flow of information, what generally fails them?

820. How it is to be done?

821. The problem with Reward & Recognition Programs is that the truly deserving people all too often get left out. How can you make it practical?

822. Are the products of your organizations Dispute Resolution projects meeting customers objectives?

823. Do you have an Enterprise Dispute Resolution project Management Office (EPMO)?

824. What specific interest groups do you have in place?

825. How can you make it practical?

826. Are the attitudes of staff regarding Dispute Resolution project work improving?

827. Does every department have to have a Dispute Resolution project Manager on staff?

828. Will the staff do training or is that done by a third party?

829. Does your organization have the means (staff, money, contract, etc.) to produce or to acquire the product, good, or service?

830. How will resource planning be done?

831. Are your organizations Dispute Resolution projects more successful over time?

832. Does the product, good, or service already exist within your organization?

833. Is there evidence that staff is taking a more professional approach toward management of your organizations Dispute Resolution projects?

3.2 Change Request: Dispute Resolution

834. When to submit a change request?

835. Will all change requests be unconditionally tracked through this process?

836. How shall the implementation of changes be recorded?

837. Who can suggest changes?

838. Are there requirements attributes that are strongly related to the occurrence of defects and failures?

839. How does a team identify the discrete elements of a configuration?

840. Change request coordination ?

841. Which requirements attributes affect the risk to reliability the most?

842. Are change requests logged and managed?

843. Why control change across the life cycle?

844. Who is responsible for the implementation and monitoring of all measures?

845. How can you ensure that changes have been

made properly?

846. Are you implementing itil processes?

847. What are the basic mechanics of the Change Advisory Board (CAB)?

848. How many lines of code must be changed to implement the change?

849. Have all related configuration items been properly updated?

850. How to get changes (code) out in a timely manner?

851. Has your address changed?

852. How is quality being addressed on the Dispute Resolution project?

853. What is the change request log?

3.3 Change Log: Dispute Resolution

854. Is the requested change request a result of changes in other Dispute Resolution project(s)?

855. How does this relate to the standards developed for specific business processes?

856. Is the change request open, closed or pending?

857. Does the suggested change request seem to represent a necessary enhancement to the product?

858. Is the submitted change a new change or a modification of a previously approved change?

859. How does this change affect scope?

860. Who initiated the change request?

861. Is the change request within Dispute Resolution project scope?

862. Is this a mandatory replacement?

863. How does this change affect the timeline of the schedule?

864. Do the described changes impact on the integrity or security of the system?

865. Is the change backward compatible without limitations?

866. When was the request submitted?

867. When was the request approved?

868. Does the suggested change request represent a desired enhancement to the products functionality?

869. Will the Dispute Resolution project fail if the change request is not executed?

3.4 Decision Log: Dispute Resolution

870. Which variables make a critical difference?

871. Is everything working as expected?

872. How do you know when you are achieving it?

873. How do you define success?

874. Meeting purpose; why does this team meet?

875. Is your opponent open to a non-traditional workflow, or will it likely challenge anything you do?

876. Who will be given a copy of this document and where will it be kept?

877. Do strategies and tactics aimed at less than full control reduce the costs of management or simply shift the cost burden?

878. How effective is maintaining the log at facilitating organizational learning?

879. How does provision of information, both in terms of content and presentation, influence acceptance of alternative strategies?

880. How consolidated and comprehensive a story can you tell by capturing currently available incident data in a central location and through a log of key decisions during an incident?

881. At what point in time does loss become unacceptable?

882. What are the cost implications?

883. What was the rationale for the decision?

884. How does the use a Decision Support System influence the strategies/tactics or costs?

885. What alternatives/risks were considered?

886. What is the average size of your matters in an applicable measurement?

887. Behaviors; what are guidelines that the team has identified that will assist them with getting the most out of team meetings?

888. What is the line where eDiscovery ends and document review begins?

889. What is your overall strategy for quality control / quality assurance procedures?

3.5 Quality Audit: Dispute Resolution

890. How do staff know if they are doing a good job?

891. How does your organization know that its relationships with industry and employers are appropriately effective and constructive?

892. How does your organization know that the research supervision provided to its staff is appropriately effective and constructive?

893. How does your organization know that its system for recruiting the best staff possible are appropriately effective and constructive?

894. Is your organizational structure a help or a hindrance to deployment?

895. How does your organization know that the range and quality of its social and recreational services and facilities are appropriately effective and constructive in meeting the needs of staff?

896. Are storage areas and reconditioning operations designed to prevent mix-ups and assure orderly handling of both the distressed and reconditioned devices?

897. What review processes are in place for your organizations major activities?

898. How does your organization know that its teaching activities (and staff learning) are effectively

and constructively enhanced by its activities?

899. What will the Observer get to Observe?

900. How does your organization know that its staff support services planning and management systems are appropriately effective and constructive?

901. How does your organization know that its public relations and marketing systems are appropriately effective and constructive?

902. Are goals well supported with strategies, operational plans, manuals and training?

903. Are measuring and test equipment that have been placed out of service suitably identified and excluded from use in any device reconditioning operation?

904. What is your organizations greatest strength?

905. How does your organization know whether they are adhering to mission and achieving objectives?

906. How does your organization know that the quality of its supervisors is appropriately effective and constructive?

907. How does your organization know that its relationship with its (past) staff is appropriately effective and constructive?

908. How does your organization know that the system for managing its facilities is appropriately effective and constructive?

909. Are training programs documented?

3.6 Team Directory: Dispute Resolution

910. Who will write the meeting minutes and distribute?

911. Where should the information be distributed?

912. How will you accomplish and manage the objectives?

913. What needs to be communicated?

914. Process decisions: do invoice amounts match accepted work in place?

915. Timing: when do the effects of communication take place?

916. How does the team resolve conflicts and ensure tasks are completed?

917. Is construction on schedule?

918. Do purchase specifications and configurations match requirements?

919. How and in what format should information be presented?

920. Who will be the stakeholders on your next Dispute Resolution project?

921. Who will report Dispute Resolution project status to all stakeholders?

922. Who are your stakeholders (customers, sponsors, end users, team members)?

923. What are you going to deliver or accomplish?

924. Process decisions: are all start-up, turn over and close out requirements of the contract satisfied?

925. When does information need to be distributed?

926. Decisions: what could be done better to improve the quality of the constructed product?

927. Process decisions: are contractors adequately prosecuting the work?

928. Who is the Sponsor?

929. Have you decided when to celebrate the Dispute Resolution projects completion date?

3.7 Team Operating Agreement: Dispute Resolution

930. Did you determine the technology methods that best match the messages to be communicated?

931. What are the boundaries (organizational or geographic) within which you operate?

932. Do you listen for voice tone and word choice to understand the meaning behind words?

933. Do you brief absent members after they view meeting notes or listen to a recording?

934. Confidentiality: how will confidential information be handled?

935. What are the safety issues/risks that need to be addressed and/or that the team needs to consider?

936. What types of accommodations will be formulated and put in place for sustaining the team?

937. Do you ask participants to close laptops and place mobile devices on silent on the table while the meeting is in progress?

938. Do you send out the agenda and meeting materials in advance?

939. Do you prevent individuals from dominating the meeting?

940. What is culture?

941. What is group supervision?

942. How will group handle unplanned absences?

943. Communication protocols: how will the team communicate?

944. Do you ensure that all participants know how to use the required technology?

945. How do you want to be thought of and known within your organization?

946. Do you solicit member feedback about meetings and what would make them better?

947. What is the anticipated procedure (recruitment, solicitation of volunteers, or assignment) for selecting team members?

948. Seconds for members to respond?

3.8 Team Performance Assessment: Dispute Resolution

949. To what degree can the team ensure that all members are individually and jointly accountable for the teams purpose, goals, approach, and work-products?

950. To what degree can all members engage in open and interactive considerations?

951. To what degree do members articulate the goals beyond the team membership?

952. To what degree will team members, individually and collectively, commit time to help themselves and others learn and develop skills?

953. What do you think is the most constructive thing that could be done now to resolve considerations and disputes about method variance?

954. To what degree does the teams work approach provide opportunity for members to engage in open interaction?

955. What are you doing specifically to develop the leaders around you?

956. Is there a particular method of data analysis that you would recommend as a means of demonstrating that method variance is not of great concern for a given dataset?

957. Which situations call for a more extreme type of adaptiveness in which team members actually re-define roles?

958. To what degree are sub-teams possible or necessary?

959. To what degree does the teams work approach provide opportunity for members to engage in fact-based problem solving?

960. What are teams?

961. If you are worried about method variance before you collect data, what sort of design elements might you include to reduce or eliminate the threat of method variance?

962. How much interpersonal friction is there in your team?

963. What makes opportunities more or less obvious?

964. How hard do you try to make a good selection?

965. Can team performance be reliably measured in simulator and live exercises using the same assessment tool?

966. How hard did you try to make a good selection?

967. To what degree will the team adopt a concrete, clearly understood, and agreed-upon approach that will result in achievement of the teams goals?

968. To what degree do members understand and articulate the same purpose without relying on ambiguous abstractions?

3.9 Team Member Performance Assessment: Dispute Resolution

969. What specific plans do you have for developing effective cross-platform assessments in a blended learning environment?

970. To what degree do team members frequently explore the teams purpose and its implications?

971. What is a significant fact or event?

972. What evaluation results do you have?

973. For what period of time is a member rated?

974. Are there any safeguards to prevent intentional or unintentional rating errors?

975. Who should attend?

976. How was the determination made for which training platforms would be used (i.e., media selection)?

977. Do the goals support your organizations goals?

978. To what degree is there a sense that only the team can succeed?

979. Does the rater (supervisor) have to wait for the interim or final performance assessment review to tell an employee that the employees performance is

unsatisfactory?

980. What evidence supports your decision-making?

981. How is your organizations Strategic Management System tied to performance measurement?

982. In what areas would you like to concentrate your knowledge and resources?

983. What are acceptable governance changes?

984. Did training work?

985. What is used as a basis for instructional decisions?

986. What are the key duties or tasks of the Ratee?

987. What entity leads the process, selects a potential restructuring option and develops the plan?

3.10 Issue Log: Dispute Resolution

988. Are the stakeholders getting the information they need, are they consulted, are concerns addressed?

989. What is the status of the issue?

990. Who needs to know and how much?

991. Are the Dispute Resolution project issues uniquely identified, including to which product they refer?

992. How is this initiative related to other portfolios, programs, or Dispute Resolution projects?

993. Who reported the issue?

994. Do you often overlook a key stakeholder or stakeholder group?

995. Are stakeholder roles recognized by your organization?

996. In your work, how much time is spent on stakeholder identification?

997. Why not more evaluators?

998. What is a change?

999. What effort will a change need?

1000. What approaches to you feel are the best ones to use?

1001. Who is the stakeholder?

1002. What is the impact on the Business Case?

1003. What is the impact on the risks?

1004. Is access to the Issue Log controlled?

4.0 Monitoring and Controlling Process Group: Dispute Resolution

1005. Key stakeholders to work with. How many potential communications channels exist on the Dispute Resolution project?

1006. Did you implement the program as designed?

1007. How is agile program management done?

1008. What kinds of things in particular are you looking for data on?

1009. In what way has the program come up with innovative measures for problem-solving?

1010. Is there adequate validation on required fields?

1011. Is the program in place as intended?

1012. Where is the Risk in the Dispute Resolution project?

1013. What resources (both financial and non-financial) are available/needed?

1014. Are the services being delivered?

1015. How well did the team follow the chosen processes?

1016. How well did you do?

1017. What is the expected monetary value of the Dispute Resolution project?

1018. What do they need to know about the Dispute Resolution project?

1019. How well did the chosen processes produce the expected results?

1020. Were decisions made in a timely manner?

1021. How can you monitor progress?

4.1 Project Performance Report: Dispute Resolution

1022. To what degree are the tasks requirements reflected in the flow and storage of information?

1023. What degree are the relative importance and priority of the goals clear to all team members?

1024. To what degree are the goals realistic?

1025. To what degree is there centralized control of information sharing?

1026. To what degree do team members understand one anothers roles and skills?

1027. To what degree can the team measure progress against specific goals?

1028. To what degree does the teams work approach provide opportunity for members to engage in results-based evaluation?

1029. To what degree do team members agree with the goals, relative importance, and the ways in which achievement will be measured?

1030. To what degree are the members clear on what they are individually responsible for and what they are jointly responsible for?

1031. To what degree does the funding match the

requirement?

1032. To what degree are the goals ambitious?

1033. To what degree are the structures of the formal organization consistent with the behaviors in the informal organization?

1034. To what degree does the team possess adequate membership to achieve its ends?

1035. To what degree do the goals specify concrete team work products?

1036. To what degree are the demands of the task compatible with and converge with the relationships of the informal organization?

1037. To what degree does the teams purpose contain themes that are particularly meaningful and memorable?

1038. To what degree is the information network consistent with the structure of the formal organization?

1039. To what degree do the structures of the formal organization motivate taskrelevant behavior and facilitate task completion?

1040. To what degree are the teams goals and objectives clear, simple, and measurable?

4.2 Variance Analysis: Dispute Resolution

1041. Are the bases and rates for allocating costs from each indirect pool consistently applied?

1042. Are records maintained to show how management reserves are used?

1043. What was the cause of the increase in costs?

1044. Contract line items and end items?

1045. How do you manage changes in the nature of the overhead requirements?

1046. Does the accounting system provide a basis for auditing records of direct costs chargeable to the contract?

1047. How do you identify potential or actual overruns and underruns?

1048. Are there knowledgeable Dispute Resolution projections of future performance?

1049. Is budgeted cost for work performed calculated in a manner consistent with the way work is planned?

1050. Are all elements of indirect expense identified to overhead cost budgets of Dispute Resolution projections?

1051. Are all authorized tasks assigned to identified organizational elements?

1052. Are estimates of costs at completion generated in a rational, consistent manner?

1053. What business event causes fluctuations?

1054. What should management do?

1055. Other relevant issues of Variance Analysis -selling price or gross margin?

1056. Are overhead costs budgets established on a basis consistent with the anticipated direct business base?

1057. Is the market likely to continue to grow at this rate next year?

1058. Did your organization lose existing customers and/or gain new customers?

4.3 Earned Value Status: Dispute Resolution

1059. What is the unit of forecast value?

1060. Earned value can be used in almost any Dispute Resolution project situation and in almost any Dispute Resolution project environment. it may be used on large Dispute Resolution projects, medium sized Dispute Resolution projects, tiny Dispute Resolution projects (in cut-down form), complex and simple Dispute Resolution projects and in any market sector. some people, of course, know all about earned value, they have used it for years - but perhaps not as effectively as they could have?

1061. How much is it going to cost by the finish?

1062. If earned value management (EVM) is so good in determining the true status of a Dispute Resolution project and Dispute Resolution project its completion, why is it that hardly any one uses it in information systems related Dispute Resolution projects?

1063. Verification is a process of ensuring that the developed system satisfies the stakeholders agreements and specifications; Are you building the product right? What do you verify?

1064. Where are your problem areas?

1065. Validation is a process of ensuring that the developed system will actually achieve the stakeholders desired outcomes; Are you building the right product? What do you validate?

1066. When is it going to finish?

1067. Are you hitting your Dispute Resolution projects targets?

1068. Where is evidence-based earned value in your organization reported?

1069. How does this compare with other Dispute Resolution projects?

4.4 Risk Audit: Dispute Resolution

1070. Has everyone (staff, volunteers and participants) agreed to a code of behaviour or conduct?

1071. Do you have written and signed agreements/contracts in place for each paid staff member?

1072. Does your auditor understand your business?

1073. Do you have a consistent repeatable process that is actually used?

1074. Are regular safety inspections made of buildings, grounds and equipment?

1075. If applicable; are compilers and code generators available and suitable for the product to be built?

1076. Is your organization an exempt employer for payroll tax purposes?

1077. What responsibilities for quality, errors, and outcomes have been delegated to staff (or others) without adequate oversight?

1078. Are the software tools integrated with each other?

1079. Which assets are important?

1080. Does the Dispute Resolution project team have experience with the technology to be implemented?

1081. Are duties out-of-class?

1082. Will an appropriate standard of care be applied to all involved?

1083. Is your organization able to present documentary evidence in support of compliance?

1084. Number of users of the product?

1085. What is happening in other jurisdictions? Could that happen here?

1086. How risk averse are you?

1087. Do you meet the legislative requirements (for example PAYG, super contributions) for paid employees?

1088. Is there (or should there be) some impact on the process of setting materiality when the auditor more effectively identifies higher risk areas of the financial statements?

4.5 Contractor Status Report: Dispute Resolution

1089. Who can list a Dispute Resolution project as organization experience, your organization or a previous employee of your organization?

1090. What was the final actual cost?

1091. How long have you been using the services?

1092. What was the actual budget or estimated cost for your organizations services?

1093. If applicable; describe your standard schedule for new software version releases. Are new software version releases included in the standard maintenance plan?

1094. What are the minimum and optimal bandwidth requirements for the proposed solution?

1095. How is risk transferred?

1096. What was the budget or estimated cost for your organizations services?

1097. What is the average response time for answering a support call?

1098. Describe how often regular updates are made to the proposed solution. Are corresponding regular updates included in the standard maintenance plan?

1099. What was the overall budget or estimated cost?

1100. What process manages the contracts?

1101. How does the proposed individual meet each requirement?

1102. Are there contractual transfer concerns?

4.6 Formal Acceptance: Dispute Resolution

1103. General estimate of the costs and times to complete the Dispute Resolution project?

1104. How well did the team follow the methodology?

1105. Does it do what Dispute Resolution project team said it would?

1106. Is formal acceptance of the Dispute Resolution project product documented and distributed?

1107. Was the Dispute Resolution project managed well?

1108. Did the Dispute Resolution project achieve its MOV?

1109. Who supplies data?

1110. Did the Dispute Resolution project manager and team act in a professional and ethical manner?

1111. Do you buy pre-configured systems or build your own configuration?

1112. What is the Acceptance Management Process?

1113. Have all comments been addressed?

1114. What can you do better next time?

1115. Do you perform formal acceptance or burn-in tests?

1116. What features, practices, and processes proved to be strengths or weaknesses?

1117. Does it do what client said it would?

1118. What function(s) does it fill or meet?

1119. Was the Dispute Resolution project work done on time, within budget, and according to specification?

1120. Was the sponsor/customer satisfied?

1121. Was the Dispute Resolution project goal achieved?

1122. What are the requirements against which to test, Who will execute?

5.0 Closing Process Group: Dispute Resolution

1123. What level of risk does the proposed budget represent to the Dispute Resolution project?

1124. What is the amount of funding and what Dispute Resolution project phases are funded?

1125. How critical is the Dispute Resolution project success to the success of your organization?

1126. What could have been improved?

1127. What is the overall risk of the Dispute Resolution project to your organization?

1128. What were things that you did very well and want to do the same again on the next Dispute Resolution project?

1129. Who are the Dispute Resolution project stakeholders?

1130. Is the Dispute Resolution project funded?

1131. How well defined and documented were the Dispute Resolution project management processes you chose to use?

1132. Did the Dispute Resolution project team have enough people to execute the Dispute Resolution project plan?

1133. Does the close educate others to improve performance?

1134. What were the actual outcomes?

1135. Did you do things well?

1136. What areas were overlooked on this Dispute Resolution project?

1137. Did the Dispute Resolution project management methodology work?

1138. What is an Encumbrance?

5.1 Procurement Audit: Dispute Resolution

1139. Has the award included no items different from the already stated contained in bid specifications?

1140. Are procurement policies and practices in line with (international) good practice standards?

1141. Is the purchasing department consulted on favorable purchasing opportunities, economic ordering quantities, and revision of purchasing specifications?

1142. Are there regular accounting reconciliations of contract payments, transactions and inventory?

1143. Were the documents received scrutinised for completion and adherence to stated conditions before the tenders were evaluated?

1144. Does the strategy ensure that appropriate controls are in place to ensure propriety and regularity in delivery?

1145. How are you making the audit trail easy to follow?

1146. Are information technology resources (e-procurement) used to reduce costs?

1147. Are proper financing arrangements taken?

1148. In case of time and material and labour hour contracts, does surveillance give an adequate and reasonable assurance that the contractor is using efficient methods and effective cost controls?

1149. Did the contracting authority offer unrestricted and full electronic access to the contract documents and any supplementary documents (specifying the internet address in the notice)?

1150. When competitive dialogue was used, did the contracting authority provide sufficient justification for the use of this procedure and was the contract actually particularly complex?

1151. Is an appropriated degree of standardization of goods and services respected?

1152. Who is verifying the performance of the contract and approving payments?

1153. Is the accounting distribution of expenses included with the request for payment?

1154. How do you deal with budget constrains and assurance needs?

1155. Do you learn from benchmarking your own practices with international standards?

1156. Was the payment made to the supplier/ contractor within the time frames indicated in the contracts?

1157. Does the strategy discus the best manner of purchase, considering the types of goods and services needed?

1158. Which are necessary components of a financial audit report under the Single Audit Act?

5.2 Contract Close-Out: Dispute Resolution

1159. Parties: who is involved?

1160. Have all contracts been completed?

1161. Was the contract type appropriate?

1162. How does it work?

1163. What is capture management?

1164. Change in knowledge?

1165. Have all acceptance criteria been met prior to final payment to contractors?

1166. Change in attitude or behavior?

1167. Change in circumstances?

1168. Have all contracts been closed?

1169. How/when used ?

1170. Has each contract been audited to verify acceptance and delivery?

1171. Was the contract sufficiently clear so as not to result in numerous disputes and misunderstandings?

1172. Are the signers the authorized officials?

1173. Was the contract complete without requiring numerous changes and revisions?

1174. Have all contract records been included in the Dispute Resolution project archives?

1175. How is the contracting office notified of the automatic contract close-out?

1176. Parties: Authorized?

1177. What happens to the recipient of services?

5.3 Project or Phase Close-Out: Dispute Resolution

1178. Can the lesson learned be replicated?

1179. What is a Risk?

1180. What information is each stakeholder group interested in?

1181. What security considerations needed to be addressed during the procurement life cycle?

1182. Were messages directly related to the release strategy or phases of the Dispute Resolution project?

1183. Were risks identified and mitigated?

1184. In addition to assessing whether the Dispute Resolution project was successful, it is equally critical to analyze why it was or was not fully successful. Are you including this?

1185. Planned completion date?

1186. What benefits or impacts does the stakeholder group expect to obtain as a result of the Dispute Resolution project?

1187. What went well?

1188. Is the lesson significant, valid, and applicable?

1189. Planned remaining costs?

1190. Who are the Dispute Resolution project stakeholders and what are roles and involvement?

1191. How often did each stakeholder need an update?

1192. What is this stakeholder expecting?

1193. What can you do better next time, and what specific actions can you take to improve?

1194. Which changes might a stakeholder be required to make as a result of the Dispute Resolution project?

1195. What are the informational communication needs for each stakeholder?

1196. What are the mandatory communication needs for each stakeholder?

5.4 Lessons Learned: Dispute Resolution

1197. Did the Dispute Resolution project management methodology work?

1198. What solutions or recommendations can you offer that would have improved some aspect of the Dispute Resolution project?

1199. Do you conduct the engineering tests?

1200. How well was Dispute Resolution project status communicated throughout your involvement in the Dispute Resolution project?

1201. What is the distribution of authority?

1202. What is the proportion of in-house and contractor personnel authorized for the Dispute Resolution project?

1203. How timely was the training you received in preparation for the use of the product/service?

1204. What data are likely to be missing?

1205. What is below the surface?

1206. What is the value of the deliverable?

1207. What is your organizations performance history?

1208. Were the aims and objectives achieved?

1209. How was the quality of products/processes assured?

1210. Was the user/client satisfied with the end product?

1211. Is the lesson based on actual Dispute Resolution project experience rather than on independent research?

1212. How effective were Dispute Resolution project audits?

1213. How did the estimated Dispute Resolution project Budget compare with the total actual expenditures?

1214. How does the budget cycle affect the case?

1215. Was the necessary hardware, software, accommodation etc available?

Index

automatic   261
available   17-18, 29, 32, 53, 66, 69, 80, 91, 113, 130, 156,
161, 170, 186, 192, 200, 203-204, 225, 241, 249, 265
Average   13, 25, 41, 61, 75, 89, 101, 128, 173, 226, 251
averse 250
background   11, 132, 165
backward   223
balance   45
bandwidth   251
barriers 45, 126, 197
baseline   4, 57, 117, 143, 156, 159, 183-184
baselined   50, 158, 209
baselines   30, 40
basics 122
because   180
become   105, 109, 112, 123, 147, 226
before 10, 28, 99, 132, 160, 166, 173, 201, 205, 235, 257
beginning   2, 16, 25, 41, 61, 75, 89, 101, 128
begins 226
behavior   244, 260
behaviors   58, 226, 244
behaviour   249
behaviours   216
behind 232
belief   12, 17, 26, 42, 62, 76, 90, 102, 124
believable   126
believe 105, 124
benchmark   187
benefit 1, 20, 24, 50, 55, 85, 100, 135, 141, 172
benefits   23, 47, 57, 67, 102, 112-113, 117, 119, 121, 139,
215, 262
better 7, 37, 47, 160, 173-174, 181, 207, 231, 233, 253, 263
between   45-46, 74, 130, 137, 147, 152, 158, 169, 197
beyond   234
biggest   58, 84
blended   237
blinding   68
Blokdyk   8
bother 46
bottleneck   161
bought 11
bounce   74-75
boundaries   31, 232

manage   29, 33, 47, 58, 64, 73, 85, 106, 123, 131, 140-141,
147-148, 162, 164, 179, 183, 198, 202, 215, 230, 245
manageable 40, 172, 214
managed   7, 30, 75, 96, 100, 172, 221, 253
management 1, 3-5, 9, 11-12, 20, 23, 32, 34, 38, 83, 86-87, 103,
105-106, 124, 138-139, 141-143, 149-150, 156-159, 169, 171-173,
177-178, 183-185, 187, 189, 191, 193, 195-197, 199, 202, 204-205,
209, 213, 215-217, 219-220, 225, 228, 238, 241, 245-247, 253, 255-
256, 260, 264
manager   7, 12, 18, 29, 39, 121, 139, 141, 172, 179, 191, 214,
220, 253
managers   2, 129-130, 139, 203, 206, 218
manages   132, 252
managing   2, 129-130, 134, 228
mandatory   223, 263
manner   87, 155, 222, 242, 245-246, 253, 258
manpower   155
mantle 121
manuals   228
mapped   32
Mapping   69, 75
margin 246
market 25, 171, 246-247
marketer   7
marketing   111, 151, 228
markets   25
Master 81
material   155, 258
materials   1, 149, 191, 232
matrices   147
Matrix 3-4, 135, 147-148, 187, 191, 205
matter 35, 43, 60
matters   226
Maximize   206
maximizing   104, 172
maximum   130-131
meaning   162, 232
meaningful   45, 122, 244
measurable   31, 39, 244
measure   2, 12, 17, 21, 31, 35, 42, 44-48, 50, 52-54, 59-60,
64, 71, 76, 78, 85, 88-89, 91, 96, 98-99, 137-138, 181, 184, 187, 243
measured   24, 42, 44, 46, 50-51, 56, 58, 60, 80, 93, 95, 188,
191, 207, 235, 243

moment 126
moments 70
momentum 116, 121
monetary 20, 242
monitor 79, 91-93, 96, 100, 181, 242
monitored 94, 96, 99, 131, 160, 172
monitoring 5, 91, 98-100, 143, 168, 204, 221, 241
months82, 84
motivate 102, 244
motivation 18, 98, 132
moving 113
multiple 144, 159
narrative 151
narrow 62
national 208
nature 58, 245
nearest 13
nearly 105
necessary 51, 63, 66, 70-71, 83, 110, 113, 120, 138, 155, 181, 191, 196, 204, 223, 235, 259, 265
needed 18-19, 22, 24, 40, 69, 71, 91, 93, 99-100, 130, 138, 171, 182, 191-192, 216, 241, 259, 262
negative 115, 175, 215
negatively 195, 202
negotiate 106
negotiated 126
neither 1
network 3, 166, 215, 244
Neutral12, 17, 26, 42, 62, 76, 90, 102
normal94
notice 1, 258
notified 197, 261
number 25, 41, 50, 61, 75, 89, 101, 127, 162, 250, 266
numbers 109
numerous 260-261
objective 7, 51, 142, 149, 155-156, 183, 205, 217
objectives 19-20, 23, 26, 28, 30, 63, 65, 95-96, 105, 120-121, 127, 175, 184, 195, 202, 219, 228, 230, 244, 265
Observe 228
observed 80
Observer 228
observing 151
obsolete 123

remain 39, 185
remaining 175-176, 181, 263
remedial 44
remedies 42
remove 83
remunerate 87
repair 177, 209
repeatable 249
rephrased 11
replace 55, 132
replicated 262
report 5-6, 51, 82, 93, 201, 219, 231, 243, 251, 259
reported 195, 239, 248
reporting 91, 119, 156, 185, 191, 202
reports 52, 91, 134, 139, 214
repository 142, 177-178, 196
represent 80, 223-224, 255
reproduced 1
reputation 105
request 5, 64-65, 143, 183, 212, 221-224, 258
requested 1, 77, 183, 223
requests 205, 221
require 41, 53, 72, 93, 168, 175, 204, 216
required 19, 22, 28, 30, 37, 51, 56, 63, 73, 87-88, 101, 130, 161, 170, 173, 190, 194, 197, 199-201, 215, 218, 233, 241, 263
requiring 134, 261
research 25, 120, 123, 227, 265
Reserve 156, 180
reserved 1
reserves 245
reside 142, 196
Resolution 1-6, 9-15, 18-25, 27-41, 43-59, 61, 63-96, 98-145, 147, 149-156, 158-169, 171-179, 181-185, 187, 189, 191-197, 199-207, 209-211, 213-215, 217, 219-225, 227, 230-232, 234, 237, 239, 241-243, 245, 247-249, 251, 253-257, 260-265
resolve 19, 22, 230, 234
resolved 130, 188
resource 3-4, 110, 155, 158, 163, 168-171, 195-196, 209, 215, 220
resources 2, 9, 17, 20, 29, 31-32, 45, 59, 74, 83, 88, 97, 100-101, 109-110, 114, 122, 135-136, 142, 161-162, 170-171, 173, 182, 238, 241, 257
respect 1

CPSIA information can be obtained
at www.ICGtesting.com
Printed in the USA
BVHW040958050719
552687BV00011B/428/P